The
Bay Area
Volunteer's
Handbook

2nd Edition

Melissa Schwarz
John Javna
The EarthWorks Group
& Volunteer Centers of the Bay Area

EarthWorks Press

EarthWorks Press ISBN: *1-879682-67-2*
10 9 8 7 6 5 4 3 2 1
Printed by the Banta Corporation, USA.
First printing June 1996

Cover Design by Andrea Sohn

A note to the reader:
We have listed lots of information and resources in this book. As far as
we know, at the time the book went to press, all the information and
resources were accurate, but be advised that addresses and organizations
change. If you find an error, we would appreciate it if you could let us
know so that we can try to update the book in subsequent printings.

Our mailing address:
Bay Area Volunteer Book Project, EarthWorks Press
P.O. Box 1117, Ashland, OR 97520

THANK YOU!

We'd like to thank the people who helped make this book possible.

Lenna Lebovich	Donna Campbell	Steven Sams
Sharilyn Hovind	Tina Cheplick	*...and the more than*
John Dollison	Cathy Maupin	*300 volunteers and*
Fritz Springmeyer	Suzan Bateson	*community organizers*
Sharon Javna	Jean Wong	*who shared their experi-*
Gordon Javna	Dwayne Marsh	*ences, expertise, and*
Erik Linden	Will T. Rigney	*enthusiasm during the*
Chuck Greene	Mary Leslie	*3+ years we worked on*
Nora Silver	Jere Jacobs	*this book.*

CONTENTS

A MESSAGE FROM GENERAL COLIN L. POWELL, USA (RET)

The Bay Area Volunteer's Handbook is part of an exciting nationwide volunteer effort. It's an easy-to-read guide designed to help you get a better idea of how you might invest your time and skills back into your community. I deeply appreciate Pacific Bell for providing the funds to print and distribute the *Handbook* throughout the San Francisco Bay Area, and I salute the San Francisco Junior League for their efforts to make the *Handbook* widely available.

Last April at the Philadelphia Summit, we launched a national volunteerism campaign, which I chair. The goal of the campaign, known as AMERICA'S PROMISE—THE ALLIANCE FOR YOUTH, is to provide two million "at risk" youngsters with the basic resources that any successful American will recognize as a part of their own upbringing. As I travel around our great Nation, I have been heartened by the generous outpouring for the spirit of AMERICA'S PROMISE. We see this as an opportunity to make compassion count!

In response to the Summit's call to action, a majority of the states and Puerto Rico are planning, or have already held, volunteerism "summits." California and the Bay Area have been in the front echelon of the hundreds of cities and communities, schools, churches, foundations and U.S. corporations that are stepping forward, pledging to give back more of their own time and bounty to the less fortunate members of our communities.

I don't have to tell you that the Bay Area is an exceptional place to live and work. However, the region faces its share of challenges in making sure that everybody has an opportunity to flourish as a productive member of economic and cultural life. Meeting these challenges depends in part on the work of individual volunteers—like yourself—who are committing themselves to a wide variety of community endeavors to ensure that the next generation of young Americans has the basic resources they need to "make it" in today's world.

Whether you can give a few hours a month or several hours each week, your contribution can make a tremendous difference in the lives of others. I thank you for reinvesting yourself back into America, and I look forward to even greater successes as your example helps to enlist others in the cause. With kind regards,

Sincerely,

INTRODUCTION

E veryone knows that volunteering is a "good thing to do." But it's also much more than that. Volunteers—people willing to *take action* to build the kind of community they want to live in—are exactly what our society needs right now.

If you're reading this, you're probably one of those people...and you deserve all the support you can get. That's why we wrote this book. Everything about it is designed to make it as easy as possible for you to find a meaningful way to get involved.

If you've never volunteered before, *The Bay Area Volunteer's Handbook* will give you an idea of what volunteering is all about... and a sense of just how vital volunteers are. For example, it may surprise you to learn that the Bay Area already has a *huge* network of nonprofits, agencies, and neighborhood groups working to help kids, fight crime, get food to people who need it, protect our environment, and so on. In many of these areas, volunteers aren't just "making a difference," they're *making it happen*. And they need help.

As a volunteer, choosing between the various causes and groups that need help can be tough—they're all so important. So we've included a workbook section called "How to Get Started" (p. 16) to help you pick the volunteer job that will be most fulfilling to *you*. It will guide you through the process of choosing by addressing the basic issues involved: your interests, needs, and schedule.

If you've volunteered in the past but are new to the Bay Area, or you just want to try a new volunteer job, you may want to go directly to the part of the book called "What You Can Do" (p. 28). In this section, we describe some of the ways volunteers can have an impact. We've provided information such as where to find organizations and commitment requirements. As much as possible, we've included the voices of actual volunteers, to bring these jobs to life. The jobs that are available to young volunteers in most communities are marked with a ❂.

At the same time, we've tried to show the connection between specific volunteer jobs and broader community issues. Working at a hospital, for example, isn't just about helping people who are ill—it's a way to support our community's health-care system. Coaching a Little League team isn't just about baseball—it's part of taking care of our community's children. Assisting a teacher in an overcrowded classroom isn't just about supervising kids—it's an important part of addressing the "education crisis." We've also pointed out that doing a little work around your neighborhood, while not volunteering in the traditional sense, is just as much a community service as a volunteer job like working in a homeless shelter.

Finally, if you're already volunteering, we've included some advice on how to make your experience a good one in the section called "Tips & Resources."

In short, we've done everything we can to make this book both a practical handbook and an inspiration. The rest is up to you.

A SPECIAL PROJECT

This book isn't only *about* community service. It's the product of a community effort as well.

In 1993, EarthWorks Press, creators of *50 Simple Things You Can Do to Save the Earth*, suggested to the Volunteer Centers of the Bay Area that we collaborate on a *50 Simple Things*-style volunteer handbook that would be given away free to the public. EarthWorks agreed to produce the book if the Volunteer Centers could find donations to cover the costs.

The Volunteer Centers enthusiastically agreed. They spread the word to Bay Area businesses and nonprofits, asking for assistance.

This is the second edition of the book, part of a printing of 50,000 copies, which was paid for by Pacific Bell and The Junior League of San Francisco. We are grateful for their support.

These books are being given out by companies to their employees...by religious groups and organizations to their members...by neighborhood associations, etc. In time, we hope to use this grassroots "distribution network" to give a copy of the book to each of the hundreds of thousands of people in the Bay Area who are interested in volunteering. If you or your business would like to help by sponsoring an edition, contact EarthWorks Press at (541) 488-4642 or Chuck Greene, Executive Director of the Volunteer Center of San Francisco, (415) 982-8999, ext. 236.

A NOTE TO YOUNG VOLUNTEERS

I f you think you're too young to help your community...think again. The truth is, young people make some of the most effective volunteers, and there are hundreds of organizations that need your help.

Volunteering is also a lot of fun. It's something you can do with friends...or it can be a way to meet new friends. It's a way to learn skills and get experience that will look good on job and college applications. And most important, it gives you a great sense of accomplishment—it makes you feel good about yourself.

YOU CAN MAKE A DIFFERENCE...RIGHT NOW

Want proof? Here are a few projects that depend on young volunteers:

• At Menlo School in Atherton, students from the Interact Club developed—and now run—an after-school program for children who live at Redwood Family House, a shelter for homeless families.

• Over the last two years, twenty-two volunteers from the VOICES teen program in Belmont have put in 20,000+ hours developing a conflict resolution training for youth, a peer tutoring program, and a stop-smoking program. They also do environmental clean-up and help out at a local senior center.

• Every Saturday, 7th and 8th graders who are part of the S.F. Volunteer Center's Youth Quest program work in 27 different community organizations. They provide companionship for seniors, serve food in soup kitchens, clean up the city, and work in museums and animal shelters.

• During Community Service Week, 550 students from St. Mary College High School in Berkeley completed volunteer projects. They worked at schools, senior centers, environmental education camps, Habitat for Humanity sites, and more. Their motto was "Whatever It Takes."

• Last year at the Coyote Point Museum in San Mateo, 62 volunteers (ages 10 to 16) helped educate more than 112,000 visitors about local ecosystems.

A QUICK SUMMARY

There are only a few things in this book that might not apply to people under 18—so if you have the time, we recommend that you read the whole book.

But if you'd rather keep it short, just read this section. It covers most of the things you'll need to know to get started. Then, for job ideas, look through the "What You Can Do" section (p. 28). Jobs that high school students can do in most communities are marked with a ✪. If you have any questions, call your local volunteer center (see p. 129). They know which organizations are looking for young volunteers.

SEVEN TIPS FOR YOUTH VOLUNTEERS

1. Choose a Job That Interests You

• Pick a volunteer job that you enjoy—or one where you can do something important to you. It will be more fulfilling, and you'll stick with it longer.

• Think about what kind of job would be right for you. What are some of the things you like to do? What do you do well? Are there any problems in the community that you think you could help solve? Write down any ideas that come to mind.

2. Be Realistic About Your Time

• Figure out how much time you have, and when you're available. (That's the first question an organization will ask you.) Can you volunteer after school? Evenings? Weekends? If you want to see where your free time is, take a minute to write out your schedule.

• "If this is your first volunteer job, it's a good idea to start with a small commitment," advises Mark Friedman with the Volunteer Center of San Francisco. "You can always do more later."

• If you're too busy to volunteer while you're in school, consider a summer volunteer job. If possible, start looking a couple of months before school gets out.

3. Consider Transportation

• Your volunteer job should probably be easy to get to. How are you going to get there? Do you plan to walk? Drive? Take the bus? Will someone give you a ride?

• Which parts of town would be convenient for you?

4. Explore Your Options

• Some organizations don't work with volunteers under 18—either for legal reasons or because they can't train beginners. But plenty of groups *do* work with youth, and a growing number are looking for ways to get young people involved. The trick is to find them.

• If your school has a community service requirement for graduation, there's probably a Community Service Director who can help you find a job. Some schools even have their own volunteer programs (conflict resolution, peer counseling, tutoring, etc.). Ask at the principal's office.

• Besides your school, the easiest place to look for a volunteer job is a Volunteer Center. Most of them have job listings for youth as well as adults. Some even publish a free guide to youth volunteer opportunities. (See p. 129 for the Volunteer Center nearest you.)

• Finally, take advantage of the resources you have around you. Talk to your parents, your teachers, your friends. If you belong to a church, synagogue, or mosque, you might talk to people who work there. "Put the word out, and see what comes back to you," says Rebecca Sperber with the Volunteer Center of Alameda County. "The more people you ask, the more options you're going to have."

5. Call Some Organizations

• Once you've found a couple of organizations that sound interesting, the next step is to call them. But before you do, think about what you want to say, and how you want to present yourself.

• "Organizations want to hear that you're interested in what they're doing," says Sperber. "For example, if you're calling a senior center, tell them why you're interested in working with seniors. They're looking for a good match just like you are. Don't just say you're looking for a way to fulfill a requirement for school."

• If you have a name to contact, ask for that person. If you don't (or if that person no longer works there), ask for the Volunteer Coordinator. Tell them that you're interested in finding out more about volunteer opportunities.

• Some organizations are looking for volunteers at least 16 years old. Others can work with 14-year-olds, or even kids as young as

10. If you don't know the organization's age requirement, ask about it. That way, you'll find out if age is an issue right away.

• Volunteer Coordinators are often very busy, so you may have to leave a message. If you reach a voice mail system, speak slowly and clearly and include all the information they'll need to call you back.

• A sample message: "Hi, my name is [your name]. I'm a student at [name of your school]. I found your group [explain where you heard of them], and I'm interested in learning about volunteer opportunities. Please call me back at [your phone number] after [when you get home]. Thanks." If you don't hear back in a few days, call again.

6. Check Things Out First

• You're not obligated to work at an organization just because you called them. In most cases it's useful to see the place before you make a commitment. You can get more information about the job and be sure you like the people you'll be working with.

• Ask to set up an appointment. "Be sure you have good directions for how to get there," says Susie Hodges with the Volunteer Center of San Mateo. "And leave yourself plenty of time so you won't be late. If you can't make it, call and let them know."

• When you visit, ask a lot of questions. Find out all you can about the job. What would you be doing? Why is the job important to the organization? Who will be supervising you? Is there a time commitment? If there is, be sure it fits your schedule.

• If you like the organization, but there's something about the job that isn't quite right—for example, the hours— talk to the Volunteer Coordinator about it. They might be flexible.

7. Make a Decision

• After you visit an organization, decide whether you want to work there, and let the Volunteer Coordinator know. If you do, set up a date and time to start. If you don't, that's okay. Say something like "Thanks for taking the time to talk to me, but this isn't quite what I'm looking for." They'll understand.

• Whatever happens, don't get discouraged. You may have to try a few places before you find a good match, but it's worth the effort.

IT'S EASIER THAN YOU THINK

*Most people are surprised to find out how
easy it is to fit volunteering into their lives.*

PICK THE TIME
As a volunteer, you can put in as much (or as little) time as you want. You don't necessarily have to make a commitment—you can do occasional one-time jobs, like spending a Saturday afternoon cleaning up a beach or sorting food in a food bank.

PICK A JOB
Many groups will work with you to create a job especially for you. "Agencies want you," says Nora Silver of The Volunteerism Project. "They do what they can to be flexible."

EVERYONE CAN DO IT
There's a fulfilling volunteer job for everyone. "Some people don't volunteer because they think it will be too strenuous," says Andy Carroll in *Golden Opportunities*. "But even people who are homebound can work in programs like Grandma Please, where they take phone calls from kids who are home alone."

IT'S CONVENIENT
Most people find volunteer jobs within a few minutes of their home or workplace. You can even do volunteer work at home—making phone calls, sewing toys for hospitalized children, etc.

NO MONEY DOWN
Some organizations even cover transportation expenses and offer free meals on the job. "These kinds of perks are becoming more common," says Donna Campbell of the Volunteer Center of Alameda County. "When you're choosing a job, ask about it."

COME AS YOU ARE
You don't need any special skills. "Just visiting with someone in a nursing home or taking a child to the circus will have an impact," says Chuck Greene of the Volunteer Center of San Francisco. "If there *is* something you need to know, most agencies will train you."

YOU'LL LEARN A LOT...

*For most people, volunteering is more than just
a job—it's an education.*

ABOUT YOURSELF

"People discover hidden talents when they volunteer, because it's a new kind of challenge, a new situation," says Rosie Caplan of Berkeley/Oakland Support Services. "They find out that they're better with kids than they thought...or that they can be patient with someone who's elderly or disabled. It also helps people discover what's really important to them."

ABOUT DOING THINGS

Depending on the volunteer job you choose, you might learn carpentry, landscaping, computer programs, research skills, or other skills. If you're supervising other volunteers, you'll learn managerial skills, too. It can be a good way to make yourself more valuable in the job market.

ABOUT GOVERNMENT

Many volunteers end up learning a great deal about government—how social services work, how the court system works, how a change in taxes effects local schools, etc.

ABOUT ISSUES

Many people find that getting involved gives them a new perspective on social issues. "Taking care of kids in transitional housing has totally changed the way I look at homeless people on the street," says Toby Gidil, a volunteer in Berkeley. "I've gotten over any fear or hesitation. I feel like I've accepted them as a part of our community, and that's important to me."

ABOUT YOUR COMMUNITY

Getting involved is a way to find out about problems in your community—and the resources available to solve them. For example, you may find out your city has a group that mediates disputes between neighbors for free...or a toy-lending library...or a homelessness prevention hotline that people can call if they're in danger of becoming homeless because they can't pay their rent.

IT'S FUN

People start volunteering for a lot of different reasons, but they usually stick with it for one very simple one—they have a good time.

WORKING TOGETHER
"One of the things people like best about volunteering is the camaraderie, the feeling of being part of a team," says Chuck Greene. "If you want to, you can even make a point of volunteering with others as a group."

USING YOUR SKILLS
Volunteering can be a chance to do what you enjoy most. If you like to bake, you might teach cooking at a group home for teenagers. If you like to knit, you can make special blankets for kids in a hospital. If you like building things, you can join Habitat for Humanity...and so on.

PLAYING AROUND
When you get involved with kids, you get a special benefit—you get to play. "Sometimes I feel about ten years old when I'm with my little brother," says Jerome Jones, a Big Brother in Albany. "We run around, play ball at the park, go to movies. My life is more fun, thanks to him."

BEING ENTERTAINED
Can't afford tickets for all the things you want to see? When you get involved with groups like community theaters or museums, you can see performances, exhibits, etc. for free. "For me, ushering is a way to support the arts and see free plays at the same time," says a volunteer in Oakland. "I do it as often as I can."

TAKING A BREAK
"I never think of my job at the wildlife center as work," says a volunteer at WildCare in Marin. "It's a chance to be outside after sitting at a desk all week. It's something I look forward to."

MAKING NEW FRIENDS
Volunteering is a good way to meet people. "It's the kind of thing that brings people together," says Peggy Propt of Community Impact in San Mateo. "The friendships people develop tend to last long after the work is finished."

IT'S GOOD FOR YOU

You might imagine that getting involved with people in need or taking on a "cause" will create more headaches in your life…not cure them. But studies show that actually the reverse is true!

IT GETS YOU HIGH

In recent studies, 70% of people who volunteer reported feeling "high," "stronger," "warm," or "calm." This phenomenon is known as "helper's high."

IT MAKES YOU HEALTHIER

Studies show that people who volunteer usually consider themselves healthier than people who don't. In one study, volunteers reported that helping others brought them relief from a range of problems, including headaches, backaches, overeating, insomnia, chronic pain, and some illnesses. They also reported that it made them less likely to get a cold or flu.

IT REDUCES STRESS

• Studies show that, like exercise or meditation, helping others on a regular basis creates a sense of calm and well-being and reduces stress.
• One expert explains: "When we focus on something outside ourselves, it interrupts our usual tension-producing thought patterns, breaking the chain reaction that causes stress."

IT CAN STRENGTHEN YOUR IMMUNE SYSTEM

• Studies show that while stress *reduces* our immunity to illness, the moods and emotions experienced by volunteers (optimism, joy, control over one's fate) can *strengthen* immunity.
• In one study, for example, people who merely *watched a movie* about Mother Teresa helping the poor showed increased levels of immunoglobulin A, the body's first defense against infections.

IT GIVES YOU HOPE

"We're all aware of what's wrong with our communities," says Nora Silver of the Volunteerism Project. "But as a volunteer, you see a lot of what's right about them—caring people, people trying hard to make a better life for their families. It's satisfying to experience what *is* working in the world, as well as what isn't."

IT STRENGTHENS YOUR COMMUNITY

Volunteering is a way to create the kind of community you want to live in, while increasing your sense of belonging and community spirit.

IT BRINGS PEOPLE TOGETHER

When people work together on something they care about, they begin to see how much they have in common. In Alameda, for example, The Interfaith Outreach Council brings Jews, Christians, Muslims, and Buddhists together to work on projects like repairing homeless shelters. "We concentrate on the concerns we share—not our differences," says a volunteer. "It makes us all feel good about living here and about being neighbors."

IT'S GOOD FOR FAMILIES

A lot of family-oriented programs and services—from daycare to eldercare—are only available because of volunteers. These services are especially important for families without financial resources.

• Volunteering *together* strengthens the bond within a family and teaches children to view themselves as part of a community.

IT SAVES RESOURCES

When volunteers provide community services, it means more funding for local improvements. For example, if neighbors help maintain a local park, the city can spend more on things like replacing old park benches or broken play equipment.

IT INSPIRES FRESH IDEAS

"Along with their time and skills, volunteers contribute unique perspectives and solutions," writes Marlene Wilson in *You Can Make a Difference*, "things even experts miss because they're too close to the situation or problem."

IT PROMOTES A "CAN-DO" ATTITUDE

"In a community where people are willing to pitch in to get things done, problems can often be solved quickly or avoided altogether," comments Chuck Greene. "By volunteering, people learn they can take action on issues like neighborhood safety or graffiti in parks—not just worry about them."

How to Get Started

Started

The Volunteer Workbook

ABOUT THIS SECTION

Y ou've decided to get involved in your community…Now
what? If you're like most people, you've still got some important details to work out. For example:

- You'll probably have time to work in only one of the
  areas that interest you. Which one will it be?
- What kind of volunteer work will give you the most
  satisfaction?
- How much time can you spend?

Taking the time to answer questions like these *now* can make all
the difference later. "The clearer you are about what you're looking for in a volunteer job, the more chance you'll have of finding
something you enjoy," says Nora Silver, director of The Volunteerism Project in San Francisco. "That's good for everybody.
You'll have a more satisfying experience…and your community
will benefit because you'll stay involved longer."

THE WORKBOOK

This section of the book is designed to help you decide the best
way to get involved—for you. If you can answer the questions
above easily, you may want to skip this section. But if you're not
sure of something…or you want to think things through more
carefully…you can use the workbook to help figure things out.

"Take your time," says Chuck Greene of the Volunteer Center of San Francisco. "Go through the process. When you're
done, you'll not only know what to look for, but you'll probably
feel more ready, more comfortable about making a commitment,
and more confident that you can really make a difference."

WHAT ISSUE DO YOU WANT TO WORK ON?

T here are literally thousands of things that need to be done in every community—from fixing up local parks to helping the homeless. It can be hard to decide where to start.

The trick is to pick just one issue you *really* care about...and pursue that. Here's a way to do it.

1. MAKE A LIST

• Jot down a list of problems that concern you (school funding, AIDS, crime), community resources you'd like to support (libraries, parks), and/or groups you'd like to help (kids, seniors, animals).

• If nothing comes immediately to mind, think of subjects that grab your attention when you're listening to the radio or reading the paper...or issues you like to discuss with friends and neighbors. What problems in your community do you think *you* can do something about?

• Sometimes it helps to think in terms of your own experience. For example, do you have a friend or relative with AIDS? Are you worried about your children's education? Did you love Little League as a kid?

Important Issues/Groups

_____

_____

_____

_____

_____

_____

(Note: Some important causes will inevitably be left off your list. But don't worry—things that don't make it onto *your* list are sure to end up on someone else's—everyone is drawn to something different.)

2. PRIORITIZE YOUR LIST

Now, rewrite your list in order of priority, starting with the issue or group most important to you.

Prioritized Issues/Groups

1. _____
2. _____
3. _____
4. _____
5. _____

3. FIND A FOCUS

• If your list includes broad issues like "education" or "the environment," it may help to focus on specific *parts* of the problem.

• For example: You might list "crime" as your top priority, but perhaps you're thinking about a burglary in your neighborhood… or a newspaper article you read about kids bringing guns to school. If you listed "children," are you thinking of babies, children on your block, kids in trouble?

• Keeping this in mind, take your #1 priority issue or group and break it down. If you're not satisfied with what you come up with, try other issues from your list.

Specific Issues

_____
_____
_____
_____
_____

WHAT DO YOU WANT FROM VOLUNTEERING?

Y ou may not realize it," explains Chuck Greene of the Volunteer Center of San Francisco, "but you *are* going to get something out of volunteering—new friends, emotional satisfaction, new skills, or something else important to you. This is a chance to decide *in advance* what you want that to be."

Here are eight of the things people frequently say they hope to get from volunteering. If any of them strike a chord with you, jot down some specifics about what you're looking for on p. 23.

1. A CHANCE TO "MAKE A DIFFERENCE"

• According to national studies, most volunteers are motivated by a desire to "do something meaningful." The clearer you can be about what this means to you, the easier it will be to figure out what will give you a sense of fulfillment.

• "These feelings are very personal," says Tina Cheplick of the Volunteer Center of Marin. "Some people need to *see* the results of their work; some need to have an impact on a broad scale; others feel productive if they help one child gain a little confidence."

What will make you feel that you're making a difference?

2. A CHANCE TO USE A SKILL OR TALENT

• Some people like to use professional skills when they volunteer. "Accountants and lawyers, for example, often find it satisfying to work for a cause, not a paycheck," says Chuck Greene. "Other professionals—like graphic artists—enjoy the creative freedom they have as a volunteer."

• Others see volunteering as a chance to use skills they've developed at a previous job, in college, etc., but don't get a chance to use anymore.

• Any hobby or special interest you'd like to devote time to—photography, opera, refinishing furniture—can be combined with community service.

- As a volunteer, you can learn new skills: computer programs, carpentry, public speaking, crisis counseling, or any number of other skills. A lot of programs even provide special training.

Would you like to use certain skills—or learn new skills—as a volunteer? Which ones?

3. PROFESSIONAL EXPERIENCE OR CONTACTS

- For students, an internship is a good way to get firsthand, working knowledge of a field, so you can decide what you really want to do.
- For people who are unemployed or making a career change, volunteering can be a good way to get your foot in the door, or a way to test out a new field without leaving your current job.
- Volunteering can be a way to advance your career. Most groups that use volunteers are happy to give you as much responsibility as you can handle, so taking on a project might be a good opportunity to show what you can do.

Would you like to get professional experience or make contacts through community service? What jobs are you interested in?

4. A WAY TO EXPRESS RELIGIOUS FAITH

- In a recent survey of volunteers, more than 70% said they got involved to "meet religious beliefs or commitments."
- "An act of philanthropy is an act of love," explains Douglas Lawson in his book *Give to Live*. "In a world filled with violence, hatred, and suspicion, giving is an expression of faith, trust, and concern."

What kind of volunteer jobs would be spiritually fulfilling for you?

5. A CHANCE TO MEET PEOPLE

- Almost all community work will put you in contact with other people, but who do you want to meet? Neighbors...other parents...people who share a special interest?

- Or you might be interested in meeting people who are different from you—people who are older or younger, or who come from a different ethnic or cultural background.

- If you're single, volunteering can even be a way to meet a potential partner who shares your values.

Is meeting people in your community work important to you?
Who do you want to work with?

6. PERSONAL GROWTH AND SELF-ESTEEM

- A deeper sense of self-worth is a common benefit of community service. "Volunteering gives us an opportunity to put...our values and beliefs into action, which in turn increases our self-respect," explains David E. Driver in *The Good Heart Book*.

- "You can't help but become more sensitive, more caring, and more realistic about the world around you when you're working with sick kids, homebound seniors, or other people in need," says a nonprofit director. "We see it happen all the time."

If you're hoping volunteering will be an opportunity for
personal growth, what changes are you looking for?

7. A MORE BALANCED LIFE

- Many people find that community service is a way to make their life more balanced. For example, if you work in an office all day, you can find a volunteer job that gets you outdoors.

- "Balance comes in many forms," says Donna Campbell of the Volunteer Center of Alameda County. "You might wish you could spend more time with kids...or with older people...or get more exercise...or be more creative. Looking at your life in terms of what's missing can help you see possibilities in community work you might not think of otherwise."

What do you wish you had time for?
How could you do it as a volunteer?

8. A CHANCE TO "GIVE SOMETHING BACK"

• Many people like to support community resources that they use themselves. "The people who get involved in parks, for example, are usually people who use the parks and want to help maintain them," explains Suzan Bateson of the Volunteer Center of Contra Costa.

• It's also common for people who've been helped by an agency (or whose family members have been helped) to volunteer as a way to return the favor. For participants in self-help programs like Alcoholics Anonymous, helping others in a similar situation can even be a part of recovery.

If a desire to "give something back" is motivating you to volunteer, what group or community resource would you like to help?

What I Want from Volunteering

_____

_____

_____

_____

_____

_____

_____

_____

_____

_____

_____

HOW MUCH TIME DO YOU HAVE?

For many people, the biggest barrier to volunteering is time. In fact, in a recent Gallup poll, 57% of those who didn't volunteer said it was because they "didn't have the time."

But most of us *can* fit volunteering into our lives. There's no minimum requirement—you can put in an hour a day, an hour a month, or an hour a year—and most organizations do what they can to accommodate busy schedules.

Here's a way to figure out how much time you can comfortably spare for volunteering.

CONSIDER YOUR CURRENT SCHEDULE

• Are there any obvious chunks of free time in your schedule? If so, you're all set.

• If not, look at your "flexible" activities—the things you do regularly, but not always at the same time: shopping, family time, reading, hobbies, exercise, etc. Could you arrange them to free a block of time for volunteering?

• Or perhaps there's something you'd consider giving up occasionally for a good cause. For example, if you play tennis every Saturday morning, you might be willing to give it up once a month.

• Often, you can *make* time by combining volunteer work with other important things. "It's not *instead of*...it's *along with*," explains Chuck Greene of the Volunteer Center of San Francisco. "If your concern is spending quality time with your family, you can make volunteering a family activity. If you take photographs as a hobby, you might teach photography to kids as a volunteer. If you enjoy playing an instrument, you could play occasionally at a nursing home."

WEEKLY VOLUNTEERING

• If you want to volunteer on a weekly basis, you'll need to take a good look at your schedule. If you regularly use a datebook, you can refer to it.

• If not, you may want to write out your weekly schedule to help you figure out when time is available. First, fill in your scheduled activities. Include anything that needs to be done at a specific time: work, classes, sports, picking up children, etc.

• Then, make a list of your "flexible" activities—the things you do regularly, but not always at the same time. Take your best guess at where they belong in the schedule and write them in.

SCHEDULE SOME TIME FOR VOLUNTEERING

• Once you decide where you have time in your schedule—and when—decide on a minimum and maximum number of hours you want to volunteer. That way you can still be flexible when you look for jobs, but you're less likely to overextend yourself.

• Choose an amount of time you know you can stick with. You can always increase your hours later if you want to.

• If you find that your schedule is just too hectic or inconsistent right now to make a regular commitment, take a look at the one-time volunteer opportunities listed in the Selected Job Index (see p. 132). Many of these things you can do with little or no notice, whenever you have some free time.

Fill in your available volunteer time on p. 27.

CONSIDER LOCATION

• It's important to pick a convenient location for your volunteer job. "If just getting there is too difficult," says Cathy Maupin of the Volunteer Center of San Mateo County, "you're not going to stick with it—no matter how you feel about the cause or the organization." In addition, the time it takes to get there and back comes out of the time you can spend on the job.

Fill in convenient locations on p. 27.

SUM IT UP

Here's a place to summarize what you're looking for.

What I Want to Work On
Include your top three issues or groups from p. 19.

1. ———————————————————
2. ———————————————————
3. ———————————————————

What I Want from Volunteering
Refer to your notes on p. 23 and list the things that are important to you in order of priority.

1. _____
   _____
2. _____
   _____
3. _____
   _____
4. _____
   _____
5. _____
   _____

When I Can Volunteer

_____ *hours* _____ *days a week/month*

What days are best? _____

What time is best? _____

How long? _____

Locations

_____

_____

_____

Other Notes

Include any other preferences here. For example, do you
want to work indoors or outdoors? Do you want to help
people in need directly or work behind the scenes?
Do you want a lot of responsibility or a little?

_____

_____

_____

_____

_____

_____

_____

_____

For suggestions on how to find a place to volunteer, see p. 113.

What You

Can Do

ABOUT THIS SECTION

I n this part of the book, we introduce a few of the causes and organizations that need volunteers—and offer some ideas on how you can help. We've also tried to give you a feeling for what the jobs are like, who you'll be helping, what the commitments are, and so on.

A FEW THINGS TO KEEP IN MIND

• This is by no means a complete list. In fact, it's just a tiny sampling of the volunteer opportunities in the Bay Area. For more ideas, call the resources listed or your local Volunteer Center (see p. 129).

• In general, we've included jobs everyone can do. But there's also a pressing need for people with professional skills or special talents. If you're a writer, bus driver, dentist, plumber, bookkeeper, computer programmer, mechanic, musician, etc., consider occasionally doing "what you do" on a volunteer basis.

• *All* nonprofits need help with clerical work (answering phones, stuffing envelopes, filing), as well as fundraising and publicity. This work may not be exciting, but in most programs it's the glue that holds everything together. If you're willing to do it, by all means find an organization you care about and offer your services.

• Job details (actual duties, training time, commitment level, etc.) vary a lot from program to program. When we've included specifics, it has been as an estimate or example. This variety is good news for you as a volunteer, because it means you can usually find a situation that suits you well.

• Whenever possible, we've included phone numbers to give you a head start in your search for a place to get involved. But please keep in mind that organizations often move or change. Some are well-established nonprofits; others are grassroots groups operating on a shoestring budget. If you have trouble getting through, *it doesn't mean they don't need help.* (In fact, it may be a good sign that they do!) If you get discouraged in your search, remember that you can always find a job through a Volunteer Center (see p. 129).

WORK WITH KIDS

*The Berkeley/Albany YMCA offers 86 different programs
for kids and families. Every one of them uses volunteers.*

There's nothing more important to our community than the well-being of our children. And all kids—regardless of their background—thrive on attention. So you can have a positive influence on a child's life just by spending time with them. It doesn't take a lot—you can start anywhere, doing practically anything—and there are plenty of groups to get you started.

DID YOU KNOW

• In Palo Alto, volunteers in the Plugged-In program teach kids from low-income families how to use computers.

• In San Francisco, the Volunteer Center's YouthQuest program gives 700 young people ages 12 to 14 a chance to do community service as part of a team...with the support of adult volunteers.

• The National Foundation for Teaching Entrepreneurship (NFTE) in San Mateo teaches young people to launch their own micro-businesses. Volunteers serve as guest speakers, teaching assistants, and mer.tors.

• One neighborhood after-school center in Oakland, sponsored by the Marcus Foster Educational Institute, recently found that 63% of participating students had improved their grades and 70% had better school attendance records. The center is staffed entirely by volunteers.

• Through Inner City Outings, a Sierra Club program, volunteers have made it possible for nearly 5,000 city kids from around the Bay Area to go on rafting, hiking, and mountain biking trips over the last five years.

• According to Big Brothers/Big Sisters, kids who spend time with volunteer "mentors" are eight times more likely to finish high school than kids from single-parent families who don't.

• The CASA (Court Appointed Special Advocate) organization provides a friend and advocate for nearly 1,800 Bay Area children who are wards of the court due to abuse or neglect. Every one is a volunteer.

What You Can Do

COACH A SPORTS TEAM ○

Background. In most communities, organized sports for kids depend on volunteers. Little League is the best known, but there are also leagues for soccer, T-ball, basketball, and other sports. "Being on a team can be important for children," says Doug Wilson, a Little League coach in San Francisco. "It's a way to make friends, and it gives them a feeling of success."

• Coaching is a commitment. Between practices and games, coaches put in several hours a week during the sport's season. "But it's a lot of fun," says Wilson. "The kids are full of enthusiasm. It's great to see your team making progress—little by little, every day of practice."

Getting Started. You don't have to be an "expert" at the sport you coach, but you do need patience and a desire to work with children. Some leagues also want coaches to be certified in CPR and first aid and to undergo a fingerprint check.

• If you can't make a big commitment, there are many less time-consuming ways to help—for example, clocking runners at a track meet, keeping equipment in order, or helping with transportation.

• If you're interested, call your city park/rec department for referral to kids' sports leagues in your area.

☆　☆　☆

HELP OUT AT A PRESCHOOL ○ OR CHILD-CARE CENTER

Background. Preschools help prepare children ages 2 1/2 to 5 to be successful in school by teaching the alphabet and numbers, encouraging interaction with other children, etc. Child-care centers may have children as young as 4 months old. Both are often short-staffed, so they appreciate volunteers. What you can do:

• *Assist in a classroom.* "This is all about giving each child more one-on-one attention," says Ann Simms of Bayshore Child Care in San Mateo. "They need someone to help them with arts and crafts projects, read to them, or just talk to them."

- **Bring in an activity.** "Preschools always need people who can come in with something new to do," says Simms, "whether it's art, music, sports, or cooking—it's stimulating for the kids."

- **Help out in a parenting program.** Some preschools offer parent workshops or support groups where parents can share concerns and problems. Volunteers co-facilitate groups, mentor parents, etc.

Getting Started. To find preschools and child-care centers in your area, look in the Community Services section of the yellow pages under Child Care or in the main yellow pages under Schools—Academic—Pre-School. You can also get a referral from your local school district or county Child Care Coordinating Council (listed in the business section of the white pages.)

- By law, a volunteer who works in a preschool or child-care center has to undergo a fingerprint check. But once the director gets to know you, they will probably be happy to help you find an activity that fits your schedule.

☆　☆　☆

GET YOUNG PEOPLE INVOLVED ✪
IN COMMUNITY SERVICE

Background. Most Bay Area Volunteer Centers sponsor programs that get kids into volunteering. For example, in the YouthQuest program at the Volunteer Center of San Francisco, adults volunteer with, and supervise, young teens. Each adult is matched with a small group of kids. They volunteer as a team at senior centers, museums, etc. Sometimes high school students assist the adult supervisor.

- "Most people think of kids as *needing* help, and undersell what they're capable of," says Elaine Shen with YouthQuest. "This is an opportunity for them to take on responsibility and help others. It gives them something to feel really good about."

Getting Started. Call your local Volunteer Center (see p. 129) or ask about youth service programs at Y's, churches, synagogues, and schools. Typically, these programs last for a summer or a semester. Commitment levels vary.

TEACH KIDS ABOUT NATURE ○

Background. A lot of nature education programs in the Bay Area depend on volunteers. Examples: At Sausalito's Bay Model—a model of the Bay in a large warehouse—volunteers guide kids through the exhibit and other hands-on science activities. At Hidden Villa Farm in Los Altos, volunteers take kids on wilderness trails and teach them about organic farming.

• "Kids love to learn about nature," says Susan Bruehler, a volunteer guide with WildCare in San Rafael for 15 years. "Recently, I've been taking first-graders to the salt marshes. We talk about how the marsh helps clean the water and the land, that it's a nursery for baby fish, and the kids really care. If you consider yourself an environmentalist, what's going on in the world can be pretty depressing. If you're working with kids, you can focus on hope."

Getting Started. If you're interested in nature and in helping kids, call one of these programs: Bay Interpretive Training, Berkeley, (510) 644-8623; Bay Model, Sausalito, (415) 332-3871; Audubon Canyon Ranch, Stinson Beach, (415) 868-9244; Hidden Villa Farm, Los Altos (415) 949-8655; Don Edwards S.F. Bay National Wildlife Refuge (two sites): Environmental Education Center in Alviso, (408) 262-5513, Visitors Center in Fremont, (510) 792-0222; WildCare, San Rafael, (415) 456-7283. For more suggestions, call Green City Volunteer Network, (415) 285-6556.

BECOME A MENTOR OR BIG BROTHER/BIG SISTER

Background. Mentoring programs match adults with children who need extra attention—usually because they live in a single-parent or foster home. As a mentor, you spend time with the same child about once a week and become very important to them.

• "A mentor's main priority is not to be a tutor, a parent, or a babysitter," says Andre Howard-Ibrahim of Big Brothers/Big Sisters, "but just to be a friend. A consistent, quality relationship can make an enormous difference in a child's life."

• This is a great job for someone who really wants an ongoing, committed relationship with a child. "My 'little sister' and I go to museums and movies or just cook dinner at my apartment," says Tamara Austin. "She adds something special to my life. I'm a **very** positive, outgoing person and it feels great to share that with someone who needs it."

Getting Started. Each mentoring program is different. Some work with young children, others with teenagers who live in foster homes and need to be able to live on their own by age 18. Most programs will ask you to commit to at least a year. "These kids need someone they can count on," explains Howard-Ibrahim. "You can't just come into their life and then disappear."

- To become a mentor, call your local Volunteer Center (see p. 129); the Mentoring Hotline, (800) 333-0734; or the Mentoring Center, (510) 891-0427. They can refer you to a mentoring program near you. Big Brother/Big Sister affiliates: East Bay, (510) 729-5050; Marin, (415) 453-3800; San Francisco, (415) 693-7700; Santa Clara, (408) 244-1911; Santa Cruz, (408) 464-8691; Sonoma, (707) 542-1546; Napa/Solano, (707) 425-6225.

- For more info on mentoring, call the California Mentor Resource Center, (800) 444-3066.

☆ ☆ ☆

TAKE CITY KIDS ON WILDERNESS TRIPS

Background. Through the Sierra Club's Inner City Outings (ICO) program, you can help take city kids backpacking, hiking, biking, canoeing, river rafting, etc.

- These trips can have a big impact on kids. "Many of them rarely get out their neighborhood," says Dave Barker, an ICO guide from Oakland. "You take them up a mountain to, say, 9,000 feet of altitude, where there aren't any 7-Elevens or other modern conveniences, and it's a real eye opener. They have to overcome their fear of the wilderness and learn to work as a team."

Getting Started. To be a certified trip leader for Inner City Outings, you need to be a Sierra Club member and go through a training process, starting as an assistant guide and working your way up. But volunteers are also needed to go along and help out on the trips, and that doesn't require training.

- For more info, call Inner City Outings, (415) 923-5628. Environmental Traveling Companions (ETC), (415) 474-7662, also leads trips for inner-city kids (extensive training is required for volunteers). And some YMCAs, Jewish Community Centers, and park departments have similar programs that serve all kids.

☆ ☆ ☆

BE A SHOULDER TO LEAN ON AT JUVENILE HALL

Background. When some kids under 18 commit crimes, they're sent to Juvenile Hall, where they may stay for a day…or more than a year, depending on the crime and how long it takes in court. They usually attend classes during the day, but they're under constant surveillance and are confined to small locked cells at night. There are visiting hours once or twice a week, but about a third of the kids don't get any visitors. How volunteers can help:

• *Bring in an activity.* Juvenile Halls need people who can arrange activities for kids between school and bedtime. For example, an artist volunteered to help kids paint a mural at the Marin County Juvenile Hall." Other people give haircuts (which helps the kids' self-esteem), tell stories, or bring in snacks.

• *Spend time talking.* "We get kids as young as eight years old in here," says Frank Betts with the Alameda County Juvenile Hall. "Just having someone who'll sit with them and talk or play cards is meaningful." The same is true for older kids. "You have to understand their state of mind," explains Betts. "It's hard to get hired when you've got a couple felonies against you. So at 16 or 17, these kids feel they've lost their life chances, and that translates into a feeling of 'why even try?' Volunteers are motivational counselors. They're there to say, 'No, you haven't lost everything. You can't afford to let this get you down.' "

Getting Started. There's a Juvenile Hall in each county. It's listed in the blue Government section at the front of the phone book, under County Government Offices. When you call, ask for the Volunteer Coordinator and make an appointment. Look around to see what it would be like to volunteer there. If you're interested, the Volunteer Coordinator will help you find something to do.

• In San Francisco, the Volunteer Center and the county Juvenile Hall (called the Youth Guidance Center) collaborate on a special program that matches adult volunteers one-to-one with youth on probation. For more info, call (415) 753-7800 and ask for Yohan Smith.

☆   ☆   ☆

BECOME AN ADVOCATE FOR KIDS WHO'VE BEEN ABUSED OR NEGLECTED

Background. There are thousands of abused and neglected children in the Bay Area who have been taken from their parents for their own safety. They often have no one except a social worker (with a huge caseload) to help them adjust to life away from their families.

- "Some of these kids have a *very* hard time," says Dena Dickerson, a Court Appointed Special Advocate (CASA) volunteer in Santa Clara. "They may move to several foster homes and emergency shelters before their life stabilizes. More than anything, they need one person who can be a constant friend through everything."

- "As a CASA volunteer, you become a child's legal representative," says Arnold Chavez with CASA in Oakland. "It's up to you to advocate for them and ensure their best interests are reflected when decisions are made in court. It's a lot of responsibility, but you also have real power to make a difference and protect that child when no one else can."

Getting Started. CASA volunteers receive 30 to 40 hours of training. Then they're assigned to a child. Average time commitment: three to five hours a week for one to two years. To find the program nearest you, call the California CASA Association: (800) 214-CASA.

MISC. RESOURCES

Every Kid Counts: 31 Ways to Save Our Children, by Margaret Brodkin & Coleman Advocates for Children & Youth (Harper-Collins, 1993). Written by Bay Area authors.

National Programs. Look for local affiliates in the phone book: Camp Fire Boys and Girls; Boys and Girls Clubs (look under your city name, e.g., San Francisco Boys and Girls Club); Boy Scouts (various local councils will be listed); Girl Scouts (call the San Francisco Bay Council, (800) 477-GIRL); 4-H Youth Program.

GET FOOD TO HUNGRY PEOPLE

With only 236 volunteers a month, the San Francisco Food Bank is able to distribute more than 3 million pounds of food a year.

The Bay Area has one of America's strongest, best-organized systems for providing food to hungry people. Over the last 25 years, this volunteer-based network has grown to the point where more than 500,000 people receive food *every month*.

But thousands of people—many of them children and seniors—still go hungry every day. It's not that we don't have enough surplus food—we do. What we need is more volunteers to help with collection and distribution, so that everyone who needs food can get it.

DID YOU KNOW

• Hundreds of groups are set up to feed hungry people in the Bay Area, but the central group in each county is the "food bank."

• Food banks collect surplus food from large grocery chains and manufacturers like Kraft and Nabisco. About 10% of their food also comes from food drives put on by individuals and corporations.

• Using mostly volunteer labor, Bay Area food banks provide about 44.5 million pounds of food a year (an estimated 36 million meals).

• They store the food in huge warehouses and make it available to programs that distribute it for free—including *soup kitchens* (places that serve hot meals) and *pantries* or *brown bag programs* (where groceries are handed out to people who can cook at home).

• In Oakland's Mercy Brown Bag program, for example, 200 volunteers hand out over 2,000 bags of groceries to seniors each month.

• Meals on Wheels in San Francisco often has a waiting list of more than 300 people who need food. "We're trying to get that number down," says a staff person. "We just built a bigger kitchen. Now we need a lot more volunteers."

What You Can Do

HELP OUT AT A FOOD BANK ✪

Background. Food banks are serving more and more people, so they need more volunteer help. Much of their work is done during regular business hours, but some jobs are scheduled for weekends. A few of the jobs volunteers can do:

• *Answer phone requests.* Every day, food banks receive hundreds of calls from people asking where they can get food. "We have volunteers who are specially trained to handle those calls," says Andrew Jones of the Contra Costa Food Bank. "It's an important part of the service we provide."

• *Sort and pack food.* All food has to be inspected, sorted, and packed into boxes. Volunteers are trained to know what to look for, such as the difference between "safe" and "unsafe" dents on cans. "Working in the warehouse can be physically challenging," says Tommy Golan of the Alameda County Community Food Bank, "but people really enjoy the camaraderie. We find that friends or coworkers like to volunteer as a group—20 or 30 people at a time. It's amazing what they can do in just one 3-hour shift."

• *Clean up, fix up, paint, etc.* Carpentry, electrical work, truck mechanics—a food bank needs help with all of these in order to keep its warehouse in running order. "I patch holes in the walls, build partitions to stack the barrels, paint lines on the floor," says "Dutch" Krause, a volunteer with the Second Harvest Food Bank in San Jose. "If they had to pay someone to do those things, it would take up money that could be spent in other ways."

Getting Started. To reach the food bank in your county, call (800) 870-FOOD. Your call will be routed to your food bank automatically. Ask for the Volunteer Coordinator.

☆　☆　☆

ORGANIZE A FOOD DRIVE ✪

Background. If you want to organize a food drive, your local food bank will provide everything you need to collect cans of food at school, at work, or in your neighborhood. They'll give you a booklet explaining what to do, posters, flyers, and barrels. When the barrels are full, the food bank will pick them up.

- Food drives are critical for food banks. "Food banks get about 10% of their food from food drives, but it's a crucial 10%," says Paul Blackburn of Second Harvest Food Bank in San Mateo. "Manufacturers typically donate things like 100,000 boxes of cereal or 300 cherry pies. People can't live on just cereal. Without the food that people collect in food drives, we couldn't provide balanced meals."

Getting Started. "Just about anyone can hold a food drive and make it a success," says Andrew Jones. "We've seen some creative ideas. One week a woman got her boss to let anyone who brought in a can of food wear jeans to work. They called it 'Jeans for Beans.' "

- For more info, call your local food bank at (800) 870-FOOD (good anywhere in the Bay Area).

WORK AT A SOUP KITCHEN OR SHELTER ○

Background. Soup kitchens vary in size. A large one, like the Haight-Ashbury Food Program in San Francisco, can provide lunch to 350 people, but it takes a production line of volunteers to prepare and serve the food.

- "We make up lemonade, put doughnuts out on trays, that kind of thing," says Sam Jones, a San Francisco volunteer. "When folks come through, we *hand* them the food. We try to be cheerful, offer an encouraging word. When people are hungry, they usually feel better after they eat. So it's a positive environment."

Getting Started. There are more than 1,500 soup kitchens and other free-food programs in the Bay Area. To find one near you, call your local Volunteer Center (see p. 129), look in the yellow pages under Community Services, or call a food bank at (800) 870-FOOD.

- You can work once, or on a regular basis—it's up to you. (*Note:* Thanksgiving and Christmas are two days of the year when most soup kitchens actually have to turn away volunteers. But the rest of the year, they're eager for help.) The atmosphere at each place varies, so you might visit a few kitchens before you choose one.

DELIVER FOOD FOR A "POTLUCK" PROGRAM ✪

Background. In a "potluck" program, volunteers use their own cars to pick up excess food from restaurants, bakeries, hospitals, etc., and deliver it to soup kitchens and other free-food programs.

- "It's a very clean, clear way of helping out," says Micki Esken, a volunteer with Food Runners in San Francisco. "The routes are kept short so no special storage equipment is needed. You pick it up, deliver it, and you're outta there."

Getting Started. Potluck programs are flexible. Some people pick up food at one restaurant and drop off at one soup kitchen. Others take on a whole route and pick up from a number of sources.

- For a program in your area: Food Runners, S.F., (415) 929-1866; Daily Bread, Berkeley, (510) 540-1250; Oakland Potluck, (510) 272-0414; Second Helpings, San Mateo and Santa Clara counties, (408) 266-8866; Napa Valley Food Connection, (707) 253-6128; St. Helena Community Food Pantry, (707) 963-5183; Calistoga Cares, (707) 942-6533.

PICK FRUITS AND VEGETABLES ✪

Background. Several communities have "gleaning" programs, which organize volunteers to pick excess produce on local farms or in residential neighborhoods, then give it to free-food programs.

- "You'd be surprised how much food can be 'gleaned,'" says Audra Morucci, coordinator of the Contra Costa Food Bank's Project Glean in Concord. "I've seen three volunteers—all seniors—harvest 1,000 pounds off one backyard tree in a couple hours. It's satisfying work. And our donors are thrilled that their food will go to someone who needs it, instead of getting thrown in the garbage."

Getting Started. Gleaning programs are especially active in summer harvest months, but you can organize a gleaning project on your own any time. Just identify a couple of overloaded fruit trees in your neighborhood and arrange with the owner to pick them. Then take the fruit to the food bank. (*Note:* Check first. Food banks may prefer to give you the name of a soup kitchen instead.)

- For referral to a local gleaning program, call your local food bank at (800) 870-FOOD. Or try food banks in nearby counties.

BUILD STRONGER NEIGHBORHOODS

*In the last 15 years, neighborhood groups have
planted over 18,000 street trees in San Francisco.*

Y ou don't have to look very far to find a place where community service makes a big difference. By doing a little work in your own neighborhood, with the people who live around you, you can improve the area you live in. At the same time, you'll build trust, cooperation, and friendship—the basic elements that make a community strong.

DID YOU KNOW

• "Working with your neighbors gives you power," says Trialisa Caplow with United Neighborhoods of Santa Clara County. "You don't have to wait and hope the city will come out and do something. Instead, you're part of a team that's getting things done."

• In 1994, for example, neighbors in East Oakland organized to control reckless driving in their area…and convinced the city to install $3.4 million worth of speed bumps and road barriers, making the streets quieter and safer.

• Every year, the Coronado Neighborhood Council in Richmond has a workday to help seniors or people with disabilities paint and repair their homes. The city provides painting consultants; businesses pay for supplies and host a barbecue at the end of the day.

• The South Vallejo Neighborhood Association has a monthly cleanup day. Neighbors trim trees, mow lawns, pull weeds, pick up litter, and so on. "We've been doing it once a month," says one of the organizers, "and each month there are more volunteers."

• "If you know your neighbors, you're better off in every way," says Nancy Carlton of the Halcyon Neighborhood Association in Berkeley. "You can share things like tools or magazine subscriptions. You'll be safer in an emergency, and there'll be less crime because you're more likely to watch out for each other's safety and property."

What You Can Do

JOIN YOUR NEIGHBORHOOD ASSOCIATION ✪

Background. In many Bay Area neighborhoods, residents have organized into groups called neighborhood, or civic, associations, which range from informal blockwide groups to nonprofit corporations. They take on improvement projects, lobby city councils, and sponsor gatherings for neighbors to get to know one another.

• "At meetings, you'll probably find there are a lot of things going on in the neighborhood that you didn't know about," says Dwight Fisher with the Sobrante Park Consortium in Oakland, "things that affect you and your family."

Getting Started. To find out if there's a neighborhood association in your area, ask your neighbors. Or check with your real estate agent, your city council member, or city supervisor. They can usually provide a contact name. Then, put your name on the mailing list so you'll receive a newsletter (if there is one) and find out about meetings. After that, you can get as involved as you want.

• *Form an association.* If there's no neighborhood group in your area—and you feel ambitious—you can start one. Find two or three neighbors who have the same interests and want to be part of an "organizing committee." Then talk to your city council member and see if they can help. Some cities have neighborhood services programs that will assign a staff person to work with you.

☆ ☆ ☆

MAKE A NEIGHBORHOOD MAP ✪

Background. It's hard to build a strong neighborhood when you don't know who your neighbors are…or how to get in touch with them. A neighborhood map can take care of that. It shows who lives where and lists addresses and phone numbers.

• "It's a security measure as well as a neighborhood-builder," says Anita Web of the North Central Neighborhood Association in San Mateo. "In an emergency, or if a crime is being committed, you'll be able to reach your neighbors quickly. It also provides an extra measure of safety for babysitters because they know how to get in touch with people nearby in case of an accident."

Getting Started. First, make a simple line drawing of your block or the floor of your apartment building (you decide what constitutes your "neighborhood"). Drop it off at neighbors' homes with a note asking them to fill in their names and phone numbers and return the paper to you. (Be sure to explain what you're doing and stress that *only* neighbors will get the map. Don't include any names without permission.) When the info comes back, fill in a master copy of the map and make copies for everyone who participated.

☆ ☆ ☆

HOST A POTLUCK

Background. A neighborhood potluck dinner—where everyone brings a dish—takes very little work to organize and creates a relaxed situation where neighbors can spend time together. It's a great opportunity to get to know people and share information.

- "People often wish there was a way to get to know neighbors. But it's not as easy as it sounds, because people are so busy," says Karyn Lipman, who hosted a potluck in her Fremont neighborhood. "You'll be surprised how many people are happy to show up to a potluck. But if only a few do, don't worry. It gives you a chance to get to know them better and build a core group."

Getting Started. Pick a date and ask each household to bring part of the meal. (You may want to provide refreshments yourself.) You can start with a couple of families or invite everyone on the block and have the party outdoors. (*Important note:* If there are people in your neighborhood living on fixed incomes, they may not be able to afford to bring food—make sure to let them know that's okay.)

☆ ☆ ☆

CREATE A NEIGHBORHOOD EMERGENCY PLAN ❂

Background. If there's a major disaster, it's our neighbors we rely on most. According to the *Neighborhood Organizer's Handbook*, rescues in disasters are made by neighbors 75% of the time. So, in many Bay Area communities, neighbors have gotten together to create neighborhood emergency plans.

- Developing a plan can save lives. It can also be a way to bring your neighborhood together. "An emergency plan instills the feeling that neighbors will be there for each other when they're needed most," says Carol Glanville of the Mt. Olympus Neighborhood Assn. in San Francisco. "When you share a support system, it promotes cooperation that can carry over to other projects as well."

Getting Started. You can get help from the fire department, the American Red Cross, your city's official in charge of disaster preparedness, or your local volunteer center (see p. 129).

☆ ☆ ☆

ORGANIZE A NEIGHBORHOOD PROJECT ❂

Background. Could your neighborhood use more street trees? A community bulletin board? A graffiti cleanup day? It's probably a little daunting to think of tackling these things by yourself, but if you turn them into neighborhood projects, you can get them done easily...and build a stronger sense of community at the same time.

- "It's like an old-fashioned barn raising," says Ann Weston with the Bret Harte Community Association in San Rafael. "You get neighbors working together side by side and before you know it, you've got something done that everyone can be proud of."

Getting Started. First, sit down with a few neighbors and pick a project. Set a date, then create a short flyer explaining details and asking people to RSVP. Distribute it in your neighborhood. If you don't hear from enough people, you can call around, knock on doors, or reschedule. On project day, make sure you have enough supplies and tools (e.g., cleaning equipment) for people who don't bring their own, and provide some sort of refreshment. Organize the project to the extent that it can be completed and cleaned up in the time available.

- For advice: Find out if your city has a neighborhood services department, or get a list of active neighborhood groups from your city council member and contact them.
- Contacts: Friends of the Urban Forest, S.F., (415) 543-5000. Peninsula Interfaith Action, (650) 343-9344; City of San Jose Neighborhood Development Center, (408) 296-8672; United Neighborhoods of Santa Clara County, (408) 295-7084; National Association of Neighborhoods, (202) 332-7766; Neighborhoods U.S.A., (513) 443-3644.

SUPPORT SENIORS

By helping seniors today, we're also helping to prepare our community for the future. In the next 30 years, the number of Americans over 65 is expected to double.

In the Bay Area, we can be proud of the effort we've made to meet the needs of seniors. Thanks largely to volunteers—many over 60 themselves—older people in our communities can take classes at senior centers, get help around the house, have free hot meals delivered...and much more. But as a greater percentage of our population grows older, this support system needs to get even stronger.

DID YOU KNOW

• In Napa County, seniors who can't drive can call the InterCity VanGo program run through the Volunteer Center. Drivers pick them up in a van and take them anywhere they want to go—to medical appointments, classes, family visits, etc.

• SeniorNet, a national nonprofit headquartered in San Francisco, has six learning centers in the Bay Area where seniors learn to use computers. All classes are taught by volunteers.

• There are about 300 volunteer "ombudsmen" in the Bay Area who advocate for the rights of elderly people in nursing homes. "Ombudsmen investigate and resolve hundreds of problems a year," says a coordinator. "They make it possible for many older people to enjoy a much better quality of life."

• A lot of what's needed is just friendly contact. For example, senior centers need volunteers to stay in touch with people who can't make it to the center. "When there's time, we call and see how they're doing," says Etta Thomas of the South Berkeley Senior Center. "But we can't do it unless we have enough volunteers."

• "There are elderly people, living alone in our community, who haven't had a hug in a year," says Susan Verde with Little Brothers—Friends of the Elderly in San Francisco. "Just having a visitor can change their whole world."

What You Can Do

HELP OUT AT A SENIOR CENTER ⊙

Background. Most larger Bay Area cities have community centers for seniors. They offer a variety of activities and serve a hot lunch for free or at little cost. Volunteers provide many of the services. You can:

• *Help staff the center.* Usually this means answering phones and referring people to programs. You can also prepare and serve food.

• *Teach or provide entertainment.* Senior centers need people to offer classes, lectures, games, films, performances, etc. "We have a volunteer who teaches yoga, someone who comes to play the piano, a woman who gives lectures on grandparenting, and lots more," says Elsie Howerton of the North Berkeley center. "That's what keeps this place interesting."

• *Offer professional services.* Doctors, accountants, beauticians, and other professionals offer their services at little or no charge.

Getting Started. This is a create-your-own-job situation. Anything you can come up with that will add something to seniors' lives will probably be welcome. Make arrangements with the Volunteer Coordinator.

• To find the senior center nearest you, look in the yellow pages under Senior Citizen's Services and Organizations or call your local Area Agency on Aging (see p. 51).

☆　　☆　　☆

BECOME AN OMBUDSMAN FOR THE ELDERLY

Background. Some elderly people who live in nursing homes can't speak up for themselves. As a result, they're sometimes mistreated. They need an advocate who understands their needs and can aid in solving problems. To help, the State of California trains volunteers to be ombudsmen (Swedish for "citizen's representative").

• This is a big responsibility. You can make the difference between someone being miserable or living comfortably. "You're much more than just a friendly visitor," says Lois McKnight, a Contra Costa program director. "You learn about laws and senior issues and interact on your client's behalf with Medi-Cal, nursing home staff, and sometimes even their own family. It's a valuable experience. Volunteers find it helps them to help their own parents when the time comes."

Getting Started. This job requires about 40 hours of training (after which you receive an official certification from the state) and a commitment of four hours a week for a year. For more info, call the ombudsman crisis line at (800) 231-4024 and ask to be referred to the ombudsman program in your area.

COOK OR DELIVER MEALS ✪

Background. "Meals on wheels" programs deliver a daily hot meal to seniors who can't get out or cook for themselves. For people who *can* cook, "brown bag" programs provide weekly groceries. Volunteers prepare and deliver food.

• "It's not just the food, although these people need it very badly. It's the fact that someone comes that means so much to them," says Bill Krammer, an 84-year-old Meals on Wheels volunteer. "My wife and I have a regular route we drive every morning. We see about 12 people, and it takes a little over an hour, including time to chat."

Getting Started. The length of delivery routes vary, as do other particulars. You can do it daily, weekly, or less often (by alternating with other volunteers). Some programs deliver hot food every day; some deliver frozen meals twice a week. In San Francisco, most delivery people are paid; elsewhere, they're all volunteers. (*Note:* All programs need help in the office.) For more info, call your area Agency on Aging (see p. 51) and ask to be referred to a local Meals on Wheels program.

DO SIMPLE ERRANDS AND CHORES ⊙

Background. By helping older people do things around the house —from paying bills to cleaning—or by providing transportation to doctor's appointments, the grocery store, etc., you may be allowing them to continue living in their own homes, instead of going to an institution.

• Pam Moyce, a volunteer with Senior Coastsiders in Half Moon Bay, helps an 85-year-old woman at home. "She lays things out on her table that she wants me to do," Moyce explains. "She's legally blind, so I help her read mail or labels, or I'll copy a recipe out of a book in large print. My two kids come with me. She just loves them."

Getting Started. A number of programs can match you with an older person whose needs fit your schedule. Your commitment can range from an occasional lift to the doctor, to a regular weekly appointment, to being available as you would be to a neighbor. For more info, call a senior center; they may be able to refer you to an individual who needs help. Or call your Area Agency on Aging (see p. 51) for referral to a help-at-home program.

☆　☆　☆

BE A FRIEND—JOIN A "VISITING PROGRAM" ⊙

Background. Older people who live alone run the risk of becoming isolated, so there are a number of programs designed to provide social contact. This ranges from check-in phone calls to regular visits. Some volunteers even wind up "adopting" the person and making them part of their own family.

• "When I first met Caroline, she hadn't been out for a year," says Jackie Ivens, a volunteer with Little Brothers—Friends of the Elderly in San Francisco. "Her apartment was dark and cluttered, there were no windows open. We've opened things up now, and whenever we can, we go out and sit in the park."

Getting Started. Each visiting program is a little different. Some ask you to visit once a week, others once a month. There are also special programs set up for one-time visiting on holidays.

- Visiting programs are sponsored by a number of agencies—some government, some private. To find them, call a senior center, your Area Agency on Aging (see p. 51), or a Volunteer Center (see p. 129).

☆　☆　☆

HELP WITH TAXES

Background. Through the IRS or American Association of Retired People (AARP), volunteers help low-income seniors with their taxes. "You set up at a certain site—a senior center, a library, a church," explains Jane Fujii with the IRS in Oakland, "and people come in for consultation."

- "Taxes can be confusing," says Jim Atherton, a tax volunteer in San Lorenzo. "Sometimes folks come in with a pile of papers all mixed up in a shoebox…they don't know what's important. I can do a return in under an hour, but I stay with each person until they feel comfortable, understand what's going on, and won't worry about it anymore."

Getting Started. Each program asks volunteers to commit to a minimum number of service hours during tax season (Feb. 1 to April 15).

- IRS program: Volunteer Income Tax Assistance (VITA), (800) 829-1040. Training is about 24 hours (usually three Saturdays).

- AARP program: Tax Counseling for the Elderly (TCE). Training is about 32 hours. Call the AARP state office in Sacramento, (916) 446-2277, to be referred to a local program.

☆　☆　☆

COUNSEL SENIORS ABOUT HEALTH INSURANCE

Background. Through the Health Insurance Counseling and Advocacy Program (HICAP), offered statewide, you can train to help seniors with health insurance problems.

- "With all the changes in Medicare and health plans, it's very confusing," says Lennis Lyon, with HICAP in Contra Costa

County. "People need help to understand their options. It's a challenging job, but for someone with intelligence and compassion, it's very rewarding."

Getting Started. This job requires about 30 hours of training and a commitment of 10 hours a month, for a year. Call (800) 434-0222 to be referred to the HICAP program in your area.

☆   ☆   ☆

VISIT—OR HELP AT—A NURSING HOME ❂

Background. Nursing homes provide a home and medical help for seniors who can't care for themselves or whose families can't take care of them. Some residents are bedridden; others can get around, but don't have much stamina. By visiting, you bring energy and interest to the patients' lives. A few of the things you can do:

• *Visit residents.* They see so few new people that your visit may be the highlight of their day…and perhaps yours, too. "Some of the stories people told me about their lives were so fascinating, I'll never forget them," says John Javna, an East Bay volunteer.

• *Bring a child.* "Being with young people is a real treat if you're in that kind of closed environment," says Diane Credi, a volunteer at Manor Care in Sunnyvale. "So I bring my son along. He brings flowers or drawings, or tells stories. The residents listen to every word, and he's learned to be sympathetic and appreciate what older people can give him."

• *Provide entertainment.* Most nursing homes offer music, bingo games, etc., and they depend on volunteers to help. "One year we made Christmas tree ornaments," says Peggy Howard, a volunteer in Burlingame. "I sat with a woman and helped her put on the sequins. She knew exactly what she wanted to do with the design, but her hands weren't quite steady enough to handle pins. She was so pleased."

• *Help with repairs and maintenance.* If you're good at repairs, you can help a nursing home maintain a pleasant atmosphere. "We have a group of college students who do landscaping," says Mary Francis Giamona of Mercy Retirement Center in Oakland, "and a couple other volunteers who come with sewing machines and do mending."

Getting Started. Visit a few nursing homes and see how you feel there. Meet the Volunteer Coordinator and find out what they need. Then decide how and when you'd like to visit or help.

• To find nursing homes, look in the yellow pages under Nursing Homes or call your Area Agency on Aging (see below). Ask for the Volunteer Coordinator or Activities Director.

☆   ☆   ☆

RESOURCES

Area Agencies on Aging provide information and referral services to seniors, but they're also a good way to find organizations that need volunteers. In the greater Bay Area:

❖ San Francisco County, (415) 864-6051

❖ Alameda County, (510) 567-8040

❖ Contra Costa County, (510) 313-1700

❖ Sonoma County, (707) 524-7250

❖ Solano/Napa County, (707) 644-6612

❖ Monterey County, (408) 755-8490

❖ Santa Cruz County, (408) 688-0400

❖ San Mateo County, (650) 573-2700

❖ Santa Clara County, (408) 296-8290

❖ Marin County, (415) 499-7396

FIGHT AIDS

The S.F. AIDS Foundation Speaker's Bureau gives educational talks to community groups around the Bay Area. With only 20 to 25 volunteer speakers, they reach more than 500,000 people a year.

Some people say an extreme emergency brings out the best in a community. The Bay Area's response to the AIDS epidemic is a good example of what they mean.

Since April 1982, tens of thousands of volunteers have pitched in to provide vital services for people with AIDS and their families, and to use public education to stop the spread of the disease.

AIDS affects all of us. We've got to keep fighting it. Until there's a cure, it's the best we can do.

DID YOU KNOW

• Educating people about AIDS saves lives. According to a recent report by the chief epidemiologist for San Francisco, the number of people diagnosed with AIDS each year peaked in 1992 and is now declining.

• Volunteers helped make this happen. For example: The San Francisco AIDS Foundation hotline, relying entirely on volunteer operators, provides counseling, support, and critical information to more than 9,000 callers a month.

• Volunteers also help people who already have the disease. "A lot of people with AIDS have been rejected by friends and family," explains Pat Curran of Project Open Hand. "Some have lost their jobs and have no money; some are too sick to go out. Volunteers deliver hot food, take care of simple tasks...or just visit and chat over a cup of coffee."

• "People are often surprised to find that working with someone who has AIDS can be a tremendously healing experience— uplifting and joyful in many ways," says Jane O'Hara, formerly of the AIDS Project of the East Bay. "A lot of people think of an AIDS diagnosis as a death sentence, but for many people it's not that at all. It's like a wake-up call...a beginning, not an ending."

What You Can Do

HELP PUT ON THE SAN FRANCISCO AIDS ✪
DANCE-A-THON OR WALK-A-THON

Background. Participants sign up sponsors who pledge to donate a certain amount of money for each mile the person walks or hour the person dances. In 1995, the dance (in March) and walk (in July) raised $4 million for over 20 Bay Area AIDS organizations. Each event requires about 2,000 volunteers.

• People are needed to get out mailings, work on the phone bank, and recruit participants. "We do tabling at street fairs," says Dan Sabatini, S.F. volunteer, "or just walk around the crowd with a clipboard. On a nice day, it's a fun thing to do."

• Volunteers sign participants in and help on the route during the walk (or with food during the dance). It's a social atmosphere. And though you're not working directly with people with AIDS, you're supporting organizations that do.

Getting Started. No training is needed, and it's not a long-term commitment. You can put as much time as you want into preparation, or work just one day at the event. For info, call the San Francisco AIDS Foundation event office, (415) 392-9255.

☆　☆　☆

GARDEN IN THE AIDS MEMORIAL GROVE ✪

Background. In 1991, some friends decided to turn a 15-acre section of Golden Gate Park into a memorial grove to honor people who've died of AIDS, those living with the disease, or people whose lives have been affected. Now volunteers weed, plant trees, put in benches, and make the grove a special part of the park.

• "The idea is to create a place where people who are sick or who've suffered losses can come and meditate or hold memorial services," says Carlin Holden, a volunteer. "Being there is therapeutic. I feel like I'm working to make the place beautiful for someone I loved."

Getting Started. Volunteer work days are held one Saturday a month. Call the AIDS Memorial Grove: (415) 750-8340.

ANSWER AN AIDS HOTLINE

Background. The S.F. AIDS Foundation Hotline trains volunteer operators from around the Bay Area to answer sensitive questions, provide referrals, and give emotional support (in English, Filipino, and Spanish).

- "Callers end up talking about all kinds of personal and relationship issues, not just about HIV," says "Cal" Callahan, a hotline volunteer, "because those are the things that people need to deal with in order to change sex habits."

Getting Started. Before you can answer a hotline, you'll need to take AIDS 101, a 20-hour basic course, then put in about 10 hours learning community resources for referrals. Most people work one or two 3-hour shifts a week.

- Call the S.F. AIDS Foundation, (415) 487-8080, or the Northern California hotline, (415) 863-2437. Sonoma County has its own hotline: (707) 524-7375.

☆   ☆   ☆

JOIN AN AIDS SPEAKERS BUREAU

Background. Many people are confused about basic facts on AIDS, so speakers are needed to talk to groups and schools about the disease. "Getting the facts about AIDS is what saves people's lives," says Chuck Frady, director of the S.F. AIDS Foundation's Speaker Bureau.

- Each talk is different, depending on the audience. "Talking about sex and AIDS to school kids, for example, takes special sensitivity," says Lisa Heft, a volunteer speaker. "But even at that age, kids understand that you're telling them something they need to know. You can tell from the questions they ask that they're scared."

- Speakers usually talk for about 1 hour: 20 minutes of presentation, 40 minutes of answering questions.

Getting Started. Speaker training includes the basic AIDS course—AIDS 101 (20+ hours)—a public speaking workshop, and practice adapting your presentation for different age groups.

- Groups that train speakers include: The San Francisco AIDS Foundation, (415) 487-8080; Marin AIDS Project, (415) 457-2487;

AIDS Project of the East Bay, (510) 834-8181; Face-to-Face, (707) 544-1581; AIDS Resources, Information and Services of Santa Clara County, (408) 293-2747.

☆ ☆ ☆

PROVIDE NUTRITIOUS MEALS ✪

Background. Several groups in the Bay Area provide food to people with HIV or AIDS. Project Open Hand, one of the largest Meals-on-Wheels programs in the country, serves nearly 3,000 people a week. Volunteers are needed to:

- *Deliver meals or groceries.* Volunteers are assigned a weekly route that takes about two hours. "Most people take the same route, so they can get to know their clients," says Pat Curran, an Open Hand volunteer coordinator. "Some people become friends, but we don't stress that. All we ask is that you deliver the meals."

- *Prepare food.* Most kitchen volunteers do prep work—peeling carrots, opening cans, etc.—or work on "the line." "Hot meal containers come down a conveyor belt, and each person has a job, like scooping a vegetable, or putting on a lid," explains a volunteer coordinator. "The kitchen is fun...the music is always on...it's a very up-beat place."

Getting Started. First, attend a short orientation to help you decide what you want to do. Delivering food takes about two hours a week, and you need your own car. Working in the kitchen is more flexible—you can put in as much time as you want.

- For S.F. or the East Bay, call Project Open Hand: (800) 551-MEAL. Other Bay Area meal programs: Meals of Marin, (415) 457-4666; Food for Thought, Sonoma County, (707) 887-1647; AIDS Resources, Information and Services of Santa Clara County, (408) 293-2747; ELLIPSE, San Mateo County, (650) 572-9702.

☆ ☆ ☆

PROVIDE ONE-ON-ONE SUPPORT

Background. You can be matched with a person with AIDS who needs help doing day-to-day errands and housework (laundry, cooking, getting to the doctor, etc)...or needs emotional support.

• "The idea is just to be there for the person in whatever way they want you to be. They may be alone all day except for your visit," says Susan Woodword with the Marin AIDS Project.

Getting Started. You'll need to take AIDS 101, the 20-hour basic AIDS course, then train for about 12 more hours. Then you can be matched with a client whose needs meet what you can offer—or, you can be on call and help clients as needed.

• The following groups train support volunteers: AIDS Project of the East Bay, (510) 834-8181; Marin AIDS Project, (415) 457-2487; The Shanti Project, San Francisco, (415) 864-2273; Face-to-Face, Sonoma County, (707) 544-1581; ARIS of Santa Clara County, (408) 293-2747; ELLIPSE, San Mateo County, (650) 572-9202.

PROTECT OUR ENVIRONMENT

In the last five years, volunteers in the Greenbelt Action Network have helped protect 600,000 acres of undeveloped land in the Bay Area and have generated over $400 million for new parks and other open spaces.

Want to help the Earth? You can start right here in the Bay Area. There are hundreds of grassroots environmental groups working on everything from controlling urban sprawl to cleaning up small creeks. By fixing local problems, you'll be helping the environment and improving the quality of life for everyone who lives here.

DID YOU KNOW
• The air quality in the Bay Area is much better than it is in many metropolitan areas. But 15 years from now, there'll be an additional one million vehicles on our streets. "Now is the time for people to work on keeping the air clean," says Randy Wittorp of Bay Area Air Quality Management. "In a decade, it may be too late."

• Lawrence Thomas, a volunteer with the S.F. Bicycle Coalition, showed how one determined person can help fight air pollution. For three years, he worked to get CalTrain to accommodate bikes. Now every train has racks for 24 bicycles.

• Before the Marine Mammal Center was founded in 1975, injured marine animals (seals, sea lions, etc.) on Northern California beaches were considered a threat to public safety and were shot. Today, the center's trained volunteers rescue and care for 600 to 800 animals a year, then release them back to the wild.

• Over the last three years, more than 900 volunteers have worked on restoring coastal dune ecosystems at Fort Funston in the Golden Gate National Recreation Area. They've pulled out 10 acres of "foreign" plants and planted 50,000 native ones.

"The habitat is recovering now," says one of the rangers. "Birds and insects are using the native plants, animals are coming back. Thanks to their work, it's become one of the prettiest natural places in San Francisco."

What You Can Do

PROTECT THE BAY ⊘

Background. Pollution in the San Francisco Bay has become a major problem. One sign: Levels of two toxic heavy metals—mercury and selenium—are so high that children and pregnant women are advised not to eat seafood from Bay waters. Volunteers are doing a number of things to reduce the contamination.

• For example: they're stenciling storm drains. The drains—covered by metal grates at curbs—are designed to keep streets from flooding during rains, but people often use them as a dump for hazardous materials (motor oil, paint, antifreeze, etc.)...which then flow, untreated, directly into the Bay.

• Cities around the Bay have organized volunteers to stencil the message "No Dumping! Drains to Bay" on sidewalks beside storm drains. Volunteers work in teams, usually for two or three hours, and paint about 12 to 18 drains.

Getting Started. For info, call The Aquatic Outreach Institute, (510) 286-0460. For other ways to help protect the Bay, contact The BayKeeper, (415) 567-4401; or Save San Francisco Bay, (510) 452-9261.

KEEP OUR CREEKS & STREAMS HEALTHY ⊘

Background. Beautiful creeks and small streams run through many Bay Area neighborhoods and supply habitats for 90% of local wildlife species. They need special attention to stay clean and unpolluted. In some areas, where creeks have been paved over, neighborhood groups are working with city agencies to bring them back to the surface. There are two ways you can help:

• *Join cleanup projects.* "Creek cleanups go on all the time in the Bay Area," says Andrea Lovejoy of the Urban Creek Council in Berkeley. "Local groups make a day of it: They take a few trash bags and pull things out of the water. If you do it a couple times a year, the creek will stay healthy."

- *Help restore damaged creeks.* "A creek restoration is a bigger project," explains eco-specialist Richard Register. "The city is responsible for the heavy construction work, but the rest—planting trees and bushes to stabilize creek banks, for example—is done by volunteers, with the guidance of a landscape architect."

Getting Started. Call the Urban Creek Council and ask for referral to creek cleanup or restoration projects in your area: (510) 540-6669.

☆　☆　☆

PROTECT OPEN SPACES

Background. One of the things that distinguishes the Bay Area from other urban areas is its "greenbelt"—the open space that surrounds our cities. Unfortunately, much of this land will probably be developed, unless people make a focused effort to protect it.

- In many communities, volunteer-based groups are lobbying to pass "city border" laws that limit urban sprawl. Other efforts help protect the land by making it more accessible for recreation.

- As part of the greenbelt movement, volunteers are building a 400-mile ridgetop trail that connects 75 parks and public open spaces in all nine Bay Area counties. People are needed to lead trail outings (hikes, mountain bike rides, horseback rides); to build or repair the trail; to work with planning committees, etc.

Getting Started. For general info, call the Greenbelt Alliance: main office, (415) 543-4291; South Bay office, (408) 983-0539.

- For information on the Bay Area Ridge Trail, call the regional office and ask for the Outreach Coordinator: (415) 391-0697.

☆　☆　☆

PROTECT THE COASTLINE

Background. The Bay Area has 1,100 miles of coastline, which includes dozens of marinas, beaches, parks, etc. Caring for these public coastal areas and protecting them from contamination and development requires an ongoing effort. People are doing everything from picking up trash to lobbying for offshore oil regulations.

- For example: One day a year (usually in September) the California Coastal Clean-up Program organizes volunteers to pick up garbage along the entire state coastline. "People are blown away by how much trash there is," says Patty Donald, a coordinator in the Berkeley Marina. "Last year we had 800 volunteers at our site alone, and in just three hours we picked up 12 tons. It's amazing to think that the same thing was going on at beaches and marinas all up and down the coast."

Getting Started. For info on coastal cleanup dates and sites, call (800) COAST4U. For other ways to protect the coast, marinas, and ocean, call the Coastal Conservancy, (510) 286-1015, or the Center for Marine Conservation, (415) 391-6204.

☆　☆　☆

PROTECT NATIVE HABITATS ❂

Background. As people settled in the Bay Area, they brought plants that weren't natural to the environment—called "exotic" plants. Over the years, these plants have taken over in certain areas, crowding out native vegetation. The environmental conse-quen-ces are severe: As native plants disappear, so do the insects and animals that depend on them. That's why most Bay Area regional parks and the Golden Gate National Recreation Area have organized "habitat restoration" projects to eliminate exotic plants and re-introduce natives. How you can help:

- *Pull out exotic plants.* Work with a crew of volunteers; group leaders will teach you which plants to pull.

- *Work in a native plant nursery.* Gather seeds and cuttings from native plants, then raise them in greenhouses.

- *Care for new plantings.* Water and otherwise care for seedlings and young plants to help them get established.

Getting Started. Call your regional park district (see p. 99) or the Habitat Hotline at the Golden Gate National Park Association, (415) 556-4353. Programs vary. Most restoration work is done on a drop-in basis, no commitment needed. Some nursery programs involve a little more training and possibly a commitment—but they're all flexible.

HELP A LOCAL ENVIRONMENTAL GROUP ❂

Background. There are hundreds of environmental groups in the Bay Area. Some are working on global issues, but many are focused on local ones—improving our drinking water, cleaning our air, controlling pesticide runoff, etc. So if something's bothering you, there's probably a group doing something about it. Some ways you can help:

• *Do research.* "When an environmental group takes on a cause, it's absolutely essential that they have all the facts they need to make their case," explains Andrea Lovejoy of the Urban Creek Council. "People need to search records at municipal agencies, study EPA guidelines, and so on."

• *Make phone calls.* Eco-groups often need to reach supporters quickly and ask them to take action. "When an issue comes to a head," says Jane Seleznow of the Sierra Club, "volunteers call and tell members what's happening and ask them to contact elected officials."

• *Attend meetings.* Decisions that affect the environment are often made in public meetings—of the city planning commission, water quality control board, and so on. "It's very important for activists to go to these meetings and be part of the process," says Dee Swanhuyser, a community organizer with Greenbelt Alliance in Sonoma. "The more supporters that show up, the better."

• *Help educate the public.* A lot of people aren't aware of local environmental issues. Getting this information out—and telling folks what they can do to make a difference—is an important part of what environmental groups do. Volunteers work at fairs, answer hotlines, write newsletters, organize publicity campaigns, etc.

Getting Started. Green City Volunteer Network, a free volunteer referral service, can connect you with over 320 Bay Area environmental organizations. Call (415) 285-6556. Ask for their free quarterly calendar of volunteer opportunities and environmental events.

• Check your library for *The Harbinger File,* a directory of citizens' groups, government agencies, and environmental education programs concerned with California environmental issues.

CARE FOR BAY AREA WILDLIFE ✪

Background. Many wild animals and birds—from bobcats to eagles —make their home in the Bay Area. But some are threatened or endangered. If you're an animal lover, protecting local wildlife could be a great way for you to volunteer.

• *Work in a wildlife hospital.* "We rescue injured or orphaned birds or animals, nurse them back to health, and return them to their natural habitat," explains Laura Pitts of Wildlife Rescue in Palo Alto. Volunteers are needed to hand-feed baby birds or animals, clean cages and aviaries, mix special foods, assist veterinarians, and so on. (*Note:* The greatest need is in spring and summer, when most birds and mammals are born.)

• *Answer a hotline.* Volunteers take reports of injured animals and answer questions about local wildlife over the phone. "Most often, people call in because they're having a problem....There's a racoon stuck under the building or they've seen a snake in the backyard and they're afraid it's poisonous," says Shirley Jensen, a hotline volunteer with WildCare in Marin. "I help them handle the situation without harming the animal."

• *Become a docent.* Wildlife docent programs vary, but all involve learning about local species and sharing that information with visitors to an animal hospital or center. "I walk the docks at PIER 39 and talk to tourists about sea lions," says Grace Davis, a volunteer docent with The Marine Mammal Center in Marin. "One of my goals is to get people—especially kids—interested in learning about animals they share the environment with. It's fascinating work. I meet people from all over the world."

Getting Started. For more information on these jobs and other ways to protect wildlife, call the Lindsay Museum, Walnut Creek, (510) 935-1978; WildCare, San Rafael, (415) 456-SAVE; The Marine Mammal Center, Marin Headlands, (415) 979-4357; Wildlife Rescue, Palo Alto, (415) 494-7417; Coyote Point Museum for Environmental Education, San Mateo; (650) 342-7755.

• *To help lost or abandoned animals,* call your city's animal care and control department (look in the blue goverment section of the phone book under your city, then "Animal") or your local SPCA or humane society (look in the yellow pages under "Humane Societies").

MAKE OUR SCHOOLS BETTER

*According to San Francisco School Volunteers, working with
a volunteer tutor two hours a week can raise a student's
reading or math level an entire grade in just one semester.*

P olls show that most Americans feel we need to improve our
schools...but are not sure how to do it.

Of course, in many ways, our "education crisis" is a national
problem, but it's important to see that it's also a local one, which
needs to be addressed school by school, student by student.

As a school volunteer, you may not be changing national education policy—but you can help one teacher do a better job...or one
child get a better education. And that's a start.

BACK TO SCHOOL

• "Every year, we get more requests for volunteers from teachers
and principals," says a San Francisco school volunteer coordinator.
"Public schools are learning to rely on the community more and
more out of necessity." For example:

❖ Elementary and junior high schools in San Ramon once had
full-time reading teachers. Now volunteers do the job.

❖ The Hayward school budget was cut 20% in two years. Now
one librarian serves 20,000 students. Volunteers keep school
libraries open.

• A few communities have formal volunteer programs, but most
school districts don't have the time or money to organize one, so it
may take some initiative to become a school volunteer.

• The three easiest ways to get involved: Talk to a teacher you
want to work with; call a principal's office and set up a meeting; or
call the PTA (they often organize volunteers).

• It's worth the effort! In a recent poll, a large majority of San
Francisco teachers said volunteers make a huge difference in students' academic skills and have a positive effect on their attitude
and motivation.

What You Can Do

HELP A TEACHER ✪

Background. This is an easy, direct way to make a difference. Most teachers need so much help that you could wind up doing anything from helping with art projects in the classroom to grading papers to designing a special program for students.

• "Before you decide what you want to do, make an appointment to spend a little time with the class," says Tony Suggs with the Bayside PTA in Richmond. "You'll get a much better idea of what they need, and what you can do about it."

• There's plenty to do outside the classroom, too. Many classes, for example, can't take field trips unless they have people to chaperone students or—if the class can't afford buses or vans—possibly drive. You can also do things at home, like making flash cards, sewing costumes, or repairing books and toys.

Getting Started. Contact a local teacher or principal's office. Some classes have ongoing volunteer needs. At others, you may have to work with a teacher to come up with a project.

GIVE A TALK ✪

Background. Students of all ages love to hear guest speakers talk about their jobs or hobbies. It breaks up the routine and offers new perspectives. Most high schools also have an annual event called Career Day, when people in different fields talk about their work.

• "Most speakers don't need to prepare much," says one Career Day coordinator. "They just talk about what they do and how they got into their career, and—when speaking to older kids—give advice about getting into their field." Any subject can make a good talk, as long as you can adapt it to the students' level.

• Though this is just a one-time commitment, you can have a big impact. "My impression is that high school students really need to be inspired," says Art Chartock, an architect and Career

Day volunteer. "They can be pretty pessimistic about their prospects. They need to know that they can find something rewarding, not just a way to make money."

Getting Started. To give a talk, contact a local teacher, principal's office, or school volunteer program (see Resources, p. 68). To participate in Career Day, call the principal's office at a local high school and ask for the Career Day Coordinator.

☆　☆　☆

TEACH SOMETHING YOU KNOW

Background. Due to budget cuts, many schools have to focus their resources on teaching "the basics." To offer something more, they look to parents and other people in the community to serve occasionally as guest teachers.

- "Teaching may sound a little scary if you've never done it before," says Chuck Greene, director of the Volunteer Center of San Francisco. "But if you're good at something, you can get other people enthusiastic, too."

- It's up to you to decide how much time to commit. You can teach a one-time lesson, a weekly class, or design a whole program. For example, aerobics instructor Sheree Tillman created a kid's movement program for her daughter's second-grade class at Warwick Elementary in Fremont. It was so successful that she trained other volunteers to teach it. Now every classroom has a weekly movement class.

Getting Started. Think about what special skills or knowledge you can share. Then contact a local teacher, principal's office, or school volunteer program (see Resources, p. 68).

☆　☆　☆

TUTOR STUDENTS ◐

Background. All students can use a little extra help. But when schools get crowded, tutoring becomes critical because kids don't get enough one-on-one instruction. "This is one of the most popular—and most needed—ways to help a school. The kids count on it...and so do the teachers," says Harold Stewart-Carballo of San Francisco School Volunteers.

- You don't need special skills to tutor; in most cases, you'll be working with the basics—reading, writing, and math. But more advanced skills are always welcome.

Getting Started. You can choose the subject and age group you'd like to work with. The time commitment is up to you. A few options: tutor once a week (or more) in a classroom; meet with a student outside class once a week; or offer occasional homework help on a drop-in basis at a library or after-school center.

- For more info, contact a local teacher, principal's office, or school volunteer program (see Resources, p. 68).

HELP RAISE MONEY ○

Background. These days, most schools need help from the community to finance "extras" like computers, athletics, or field trips. Sometimes they even need help buying basic supplies like pencils and paper! A couple of things you can do:

- *Participate in school fairs, bake sales, raffles, etc.* These fund-raising events bring in thousands of dollars. You can make flyers, sell refreshments, help organize—whatever you have time for.

- *Solicit money or supplies.* Schools (and individual classrooms) need everything from scissors to computers, but few teachers have time to go into the community and plead their case. You can do it for them. You might even be able to get a local business or group to "adopt" the school and cover certain expenses on an ongoing basis.

Getting Started. To find a class to support, talk to teachers directly or ask the principal's office who needs help. Then ask the teacher to make a "wish list," including approximate costs and priorities.

WORK IN A SCHOOL OFFICE ✪

Background. Like every organization, schools need office support to keep running. Things you can do:

• *Help in the administrative office.* Volunteers can copy flyers and worksheets, update student files, make attendance calls, etc. If you enjoy this kind of work, you can do it on a regular basis, or you can just put in a few hours when something special comes up.

• *Work in a nurse's office or library.* With budget cutbacks, some nurses and librarians work in three or four different schools at once—which means they're in each location only once a week. Volunteers keep the nurse's office open and call parents or a doctor if necessary. In libraries, they help students and put books away. If you can, it's helpful to commit to a shift a week, so the school can create a schedule.

Getting Started. Contact a local school and ask what they need.

☆　　☆　　☆

ASSIST WITH SCHOOL SPORTS AND RECREATION ✪

Background. Some schools couldn't have a sports program without volunteer athletic coaches. Others just need extra adults around to supervise students on the playground or in the school gym.

• Dick Nelson goes to Bayside Middle School in San Mateo during lunch period once a week and supervises the weight room. "I see these kids in my hardware store or on the street, and this gives me a chance to get to know them," he says. "I show them how to use the equipment, spot for them...but we also talk about things going on in their lives. Some of these kids don't have a man around; they need adults who know them and can talk to them."

Getting Started. If you can't make a regular commitment, there are lots of ways to help on an occasional basis. Coaching is a bigger job, requiring several hours a week during the season.

• For more information, contact a local teacher, principal's office, school sports department, or school volunteer program (see Resources, p. 68).

FIX UP A SCHOOL ✪

Background. Many Bay Area schools have little money for maintenance, let alone improvements. They depend on people in the
community to do things like paint classrooms, mow lawns, set up
playground equipment, and more.

> • "Our big project right now is putting in new fields for softball
> and baseball—the previous field was just dirt and weeds," says
> Marty Hronec, president of the Booster Club for Casa Grande
> High School in Petaluma. "It's important that kids have a clean,
> safe play area and feel proud of their school."

Getting Started. Schools and PTA groups usually organize Saturday workdays for maintenance projects. "We recently had 150
people work at one of our junior high schools," says Barbara Bow-
man with Berkeley School Volunteers. "They built a retaining
wall, painted the gym, and planted trees. With that many people,
you can do a lot in one day."

> • Contact a local teacher, principal's office, or school volunteer
> program (see Resources, below) and ask about workdays.

RESOURCES

School Volunteer Programs. Some Bay Area communities have
formal school volunteer programs:

- San Francisco School Volunteers, (415) 274-0250
- Berkeley School Volunteers, (510) 644-8833
- Oakland: Marcus Foster Educational Institute, (510) 835-8477
- Partners in Education of Contra Costa County, Regional
  Occupation Program, (510) 942-3448
- Marin County Office of Education Volunteer Referral
  Program, (415) 499-5811
- Marin Communities in Schools, (415) 257-3092
- Napa County: Special Education, (707) 253-6807; Court
  Community Schools, (707) 253-6830
- Petaluma School Volunteers Program, (707) 778-4617
- San Mateo County: Volunteer Center, (650) 373-4634
- Santa Clara County: Volunteer Exchange, (408) 247-1126

CUT DOWN ON CRIME & VIOLENCE

*In a recent public opinion poll, Bay Area residents
ranked crime as our #1 or #2 biggest problem.*

Most law-enforcement officials will tell you that it's impossible to stop crime without community involvement and support.

Although we don't usually think of crime fighting as a volunteer job, there are a surprising number of effective things that citizens can do to help reduce crime and violence.

DID YOU KNOW

• Police stations often make use of volunteer labor. In the Marin County Sheriff's office, for example, volunteers input data from about 20,000 field interrogations a year, which helps police find criminals faster.

• Volunteers who answer the Talkline of the Family Service Agency in San Francisco help prevent child abuse by handling more than 2,500 calls a month from stressed parents.

• Neighbors who form "crimewatch" groups receive training in crime prevention and agree to look out for each others' safety and property. Results are impressive: On average, residential crime is reduced by over 40%. One group in Orinda cut local crime by 76%.

• Neighbors in the Roosevelt Park area of San Jose worked with police to combat "blatant drug dealing and high crime rates." They closed troublesome bars and nightclubs and set up programs for local kids. From 1991 to 1995, there were 2,225 fewer crimes reported than in the previous four years.

• Even working with convicted criminals has been shown to reduce crime. According to the National Prison Project, offenders who participate in support programs as inmates, or after their release, have a much lower return-to-crime rate. "When a volunteer cares enough to tutor or visit them," says Judy Evans of Friends Outside in San Jose, "it can make a real difference."

What You Can Do

JOIN—OR START—A CRIMEWATCH GROUP

Background. All around the Bay Area, neighbors who are fed up with crime have gotten together to form "crimewatch groups." They agree to keep an eye on each others' homes, invite police officers to talk about personal security, set up "citizen patrols," and do other things that help prevent crime.

- If there's no group in your area, you can get one going. "Think of yourself in a leadership role," says Mike Rogers with Hayward Neighborhood Alert. "Go to people and say, 'Let's see what we can do about this!' You shouldn't have much trouble recruiting supporters. If *you're* concerned about crime, your neighbors probably feel the same way."

Getting Started. If you're joining a group, your commitment can be as small as going to an occasional meeting. Starting one can be as simple as getting a few interested neighbors together and asking a police officer to come talk with you. At the very least, you'll get to know your neighbors and learn to make yourself and your house "hard targets."

- *To find out if there's a group near you,* ask your neighbors or call the local police station. Ask for the "community services division" or the "crime-prevention unit."

- *For more information about starting a crimewatch group:*

  ❖ S.A.F.E. (Safety Awareness for Everyone) serves primarily San Francisco residents but offers limited assistance to other Bay Area groups: (415) 553-1984.

  ❖ National Assn. of Town Watch, 7 Wynnewood Rd., Suite 215, Wynnewood, PA 19096, (610) 649-7055. An information clearinghouse.

  ❖ National Crime Prevention Council, 1700 K St., NW, 2nd Floor, Washington, D.C. 20006, (202) 466-6272. Publishes materials; can refer you to local groups who serve as consultants.

  ❖ Further reading: *Safe Homes, Safe Neighborhoods: Stopping Crime Where You Live* by Stephanie Mann with M. C. Blakeman. (Nolo Press, 1993). To order, call (800) 955-4775.

HELP OUT POLICE AND SHERIFF DEPARTMENTS

Background. You may be surprised to hear that volunteers are needed in law enforcement agencies. But "so much of crime prevention and capturing criminals goes on behind the scenes," says Joan Brown of Marin Civic Volunteers, "there's a lot volunteers can do. Every hour they give frees up police officers to do more work in the field."

• Volunteer jobs in law enforcement can be quite interesting. One example: Frank Hansen, a volunteer at the Marin County Sheriff's Department, works in crime analysis, entering information into the computer. "We keep records of crimes and people who are arrested, so when a new crime is committed, the police can see if it matches past crimes," he explains. "A lot of crimes are solved that way. I figure maybe I'm preventing more crimes from taking place, and that's gratifying to me."

Getting Started. Call your police department and ask if they have a volunteer program (not all do). If there's no program, they may still be interested in working with you to create a job. Suggest it.

HELP INMATES OR EX-OFFENDERS WHO WANT TO CHANGE

Background. Unfortunately, most prisons don't focus their resources on rehabilitation. But volunteers can help people who are trying to turn their lives around. Here are a few ways you can reduce the chance that someone will continue a life of crime:

• *Tutor inmates.* Studies show that 40% of state prisoners can't read and only 38% have a high school diploma. Not only are inmates with a diploma more likely to get a job when they get out, says Judy Evans with Friends Outside in San Jose, "just the sense of accomplishment it gives someone can make a difference." Most prisons and jails have literacy and GED programs.

• *Be a pen pal.* If you don't feel comfortable visiting a jail or prison, you can still help an inmate by writing letters. "I've been writing to a young man in jail for almost three years," says a volunteer in Berkeley. "I send him books and then we discuss them in our letters. We've gotten to be friends. He says it means a lot to him to have someone listen and encourage him."

• *Help ex-offenders make the transition back into society.*
Through programs like Friends Outside, ex-offenders can get
help from volunteers with everything from filling out job applications to finding affordable housing and clothes.

Getting Started. It's natural to have reservations about working
with inmates or ex-offenders. But don't make up your mind before you get the facts. Many people find this work very rewarding, and programs are structured to make sure volunteers are safe.
If interested, call one of the groups listed below. They can answer your questions and give you a better idea of what to expect:

• Friends Outside, main office, San Jose, (408) 985-8807; Santa Clara County, (408) 295-6033; Contra Costa County, (510)
228-0644

• The Northern California Service League, San Francisco
County, (415) 552-9250; San Mateo Service League, (415) 364-
4664; The House at San Quentin, San Rafael, (415) 456-4200;
Centerforce, San Rafael, (415) 456-9980. Or contact local
prisons directly. Ask for the Volunteer Coordinator.

☆　☆　☆

WORK IN A SHELTER FOR BATTERED WOMEN

Background. A shelter, or "safe house," is a place where battered
women and children can stay. It can be their best chance of es-
caping violence and gives them the opportunity to create a new
life for themselves. As a volunteer, you can help shelters serve
their clients by answering a crisis hotline, cooking, accompanying women to court, babysitting, etc.

• "Some shelter volunteers have experienced abuse themselves, so they understand the issues involved," says Magdalena
Cosentino of Safe Place in Oakland. "But that's by no means a
prerequisite. Above all, shelters need people who are caring and
compassionate."

Getting Started. Look for shelters in the Community Services
section of the yellow pages under Child Abuse and Family
Violence. Volunteer opportunities vary. If you want to work di-

rectly with clients, you'll need 40+ hours of training. Other jobs, like working in the office, don't require any training. However, all jobs do require a fingerprint check. (*Note*: Not all battered women shelters use male volunteers, but many welcome the opportunity to provide a positive male role model for the kids.)

☆　☆　☆

HELP BATTERERS CHANGE

Background. "Many people don't realize how much pain men who are violent are in, how desperate they are to get out of that cycle," says Rich Yurman, a volunteer with Men Overcoming Violence (MOVE) in San Francisco.

• To address this problem, groups have formed to counsel men who have been violent, with the underlying goal of helping them change their view of masculinity. These programs usually need volunteers to answer calls, give talks in schools, and co-facilitate support groups.

• "Most men are pretty ambivalent about volunteering for this kind of work," says John Beem of MOVE, "because it invites them to face up to male behavior in our society. But for those who can do that, it's a great opportunity to combat the problem."

Getting Started. To work with clients or answer phones, you'll need to go through a training program and learn about domestic violence issues. Groups provide the training in exchange for a commitment. There are also some jobs that don't require training. (*Note*: About half the volunteers at MOVE are women.)

• For info or referral, contact MOVE, (415) 777-4496; Battered Women's Alternatives, Men's Program, Concord, (510) 676-2845; The Family Institute of Psychosynthesis, Redwood City, (415) 365-1616; or Marin Abused Women's Services, Men's Program, San Rafael, (415) 457-6760.

☆　☆　☆

HELP PREVENT CHILD ABUSE

Background. Every year in the Bay Area, there are more than 100,000 reported incidents of child abuse or neglect. Fortunately, there are programs designed to prevent such abuse by offering education, support for stressed parents, and workshops for kids. How you can help:

- *Join a speaker's bureau.* A prevention program can train you to give presentations to community groups, parents groups, etc., on issues surrounding child abuse. "This used to be a taboo subject," says Norma Rodriguez, of Child Assault Prevention (CAP) in Oakland. "But we're learning that the best way to prevent abuse is to make it a public issue and educate people."

- *Answer a hotline.* There are 24-hour "parental stress" hotlines throughout the Bay Area, staffed mostly by volunteers. "People can call us when they're frustrated or angry...instead of taking it out on their kids," says Liz Weed, a volunteer with Talkline, a hotline in San Francisco. "Some people I talk to every week, so they know I'm there for them."

- *Work with kids in prevention programs.* If you like working with kids, you could help conduct child abuse-prevention workshops in schools, as a facilitator's aid. "You participate in role-playing and help keep the kids focused," explains Nancy Brady, a CAP volunteer. "You're preventing kids from getting into an unsafe situation, helping them understand that they have rights, that they can stick up for themselves." (*Note*: Not all prevention programs use volunteers in classrooms.)

Getting Started. To be a speaker, answer a hotline, or work with kids takes at least 30 hours of training. Commitment levels vary.

- To find child abuse-prevention programs in your area, call your county Child Abuse Council. Each county also has a Family Service Agency, Family Stress Center, or Parental Stress Center working to prevent child abuse. Look in the Community Services section of the yellow pages under Child Abuse and Family Violence. Child Abuse Prevention in Oakland, (510) 893-5444; Talkline in S.F., (415) 387-3684. In San Mateo County, call Youth and Family Assistance, (650) 366-8401, or Child Abuse Prevention Center, (650) 327-8120.

TACKLE HOUSING AND HOMELESSNESS

There are an estimated 234,000 homeless people in the Bay Area—about a third of them are parents and children.

Having a decent place to live is a basic human need. Yet thousands of people in the Bay Area are living without a roof over their heads…and many more are in danger of losing their homes.

If you want to help, there are hundreds of organizations you can work with. Once someone has lost everything, it can be hard for them to get back on their feet, but people do turn their lives around—and often it's a volunteer in the right place, at the right time, who makes that possible.

DID YOU KNOW

• A growing number of people in our cities have nowhere to live. But most of them aren't on the street. They're the "invisible" homeless: people staying with family or friends…living in cars…or barely holding onto a temporary room.

• These people rely on community services to get by: soup kitchens, free clinics, and—as a last resort—shelters. To improve their situation, they look to adult education programs, treatment centers, and housing facilities where they can live while they save money for an apartment.

• But the amount of available assistance depends on volunteers. For example, with 35 volunteers working two to three hours a week, an emergency shelter in San Mateo provides a bed, shower, and two meals for 140 people each night. "With just one more person, we could offer a job-training class," says the director. "That's what *really* helps people get off the street."

• "If you help just *one* homeless person, it makes a difference," says Donna Campbell of the Volunteer Center of Alameda. "Say that person gets a job, instead of being hungry and moving from place to place, and their kids grow up more secure, going to school, and learning to read and write. That's a huge change."

What You Can Do

HELP AT A SHELTER OR DROP-IN CENTER ⊗

Background. Shelters are a lifeline to people who have nowhere to go, providing a temporary place to sleep and—in some cases—a meal and a shower. Some are for women only, some are for men, a few serve families, some are open only in the winter. "Drop-in centers" provide homeless people (especially women and children) with a place to go during the day, so they don't have to stay on the street while shelters are closed. They offer food, referrals, and counseling. Volunteers can help in a number of ways:

• *Be an attendant.* Sign people in, hand out towels and blankets (in a shelter), and show newcomers where to find food or a shower.

• *Offer referrals.* Learn about services available in the community and help people find what they need—food, medical care, classes, etc. In a drop-in center, this could include staying in touch with clients and counseling them on an ongoing basis.

• *Cook or serve food.* Most shelters and drop-in centers offer at least one meal a day. In large shelters, professional cooks usually plan meals, and volunteers serve or do prep work (peeling carrots, etc.). In smaller places, volunteers and clients may cook and eat together.

• *Help maintain the shelter or center.* This may mean working with a group on a one-time project, like painting a building. Or, if you're particularly handy, you might help on an ongoing basis. "I was a sign painter," says Eduardo Ruiz, a shelter volunteer. "Now I'm retired, so I go by every other day and do whatever needs to be done—fix file cabinets, paint, put up pictures. I'm also Santa Claus at Christmastime."

Getting Started. At most shelters, you have choices about what to do. You can work directly with homeless people or work "behind the scenes." As much as they can, the staff will work with you to find something that fits your schedule and interests.

• Look for local shelters and centers in the Community Services section of the yellow pages, call your county's Homeless Coalition (see p. 81), or contact a Volunteer Center (see p. 129).

BABYSIT HOMELESS CHILDREN ✪

Background. For homeless parents, being able to leave their children in a safe place for a few hours can be a big relief. It gives them a chance to take a break, go to a workshop, study for their GED, or work on something else that will improve their long-range situation.

- For the kids, being with volunteers is a special play time. "We try to give all the kids a chance to run around and get silly, not just watch TV," says Toby Gidal, a babysitter. "We play make-believe with the younger children and sing songs. Their parents usually have more practical things to worry about, so they aren't as able to do that."

Getting Started. Child care is offered in a lot of different places—shelters, drop-in centers, transitional housing facilities, etc. You'll need to go through a background check first, but once an organization knows you, they're usually flexible about scheduling.

- Call local homeless support organizations, your county Homeless Coalition (see p. 81), or a Volunteer Center (see p. 129) for referral to child-care programs.

TUTOR HOMELESS ADULTS

Background. Many homeless support organizations offer adult education classes or refer clients to nearby adult schools. Tutors are always needed to provide extra help in class or study rooms.

- This often isn't tutoring in the traditional sense. "The main thing is not so much what people learn, but the self-esteem it gives them," says Hamilton Hunt, who runs a computer lab. "Knowing they *can* learn to use a computer if they want to is a good feeling." In some programs you may be helping people write resumes, get an ID card, or work on other "life skills."

Getting Started. Call local homeless organizations, your county Homeless Coalition (see p. 81), or a Volunteer Center (see p. 129) and ask where to find nearby education programs for homeless adults. If they refer you to an adult school, ask for the Basic Education Coordinator. Commitment levels vary.

TUTOR HOMELESS KIDS ⊙

Background. Studies show that about a third of all homeless kids don't attend school regularly. Spending a few hours with a tutor once a week can give them the extra help they need to keep up—as well as much-needed emotional support.

• "Education is important, but to these kids it's not about 'two plus two,'" says Sheri Dean, a volunteer tutor. "They just want someone to pat them on the shoulder and say 'how's it going?'"

Getting Started. Tutoring programs try to provide as much continuity for the kids as possible, so they often ask volunteers to commit to working a couple hours a week, especially if they're matched with one child. Since the kids are homeless, though, there's no guarantee that they can make a commitment in return. Be prepared to be flexible.

• Tutoring programs for homeless kids are offered in a variety of places—drop-in centers, transitional housing facilities, sometimes larger shelters. Call local homeless organizations, your county Homeless Coalition (see p. 81), or a Volunteer Center (see p. 129) for a referral.

☆ ☆ ☆

ANSWER A HOMELESSNESS PREVENTION HOTLINE

Background. You've probably heard that people on a limited income are often one emergency away from being homeless. Homelessness prevention hotlines help folks stay afloat by telling them where to find services.

• "If someone hasn't asked for help before, they don't realize what's available in the community," says Dorothy Wright, a Helpline volunteer. "They may be eligible for rental assistance, medical help, a free food box. You're there to talk the problem through with them and give them encouragement. It's inspiring to see the courage people come up with when they have a little support."

Getting Started. To answer a homelessness prevention hotline, you'll need a thorough knowledge of community resources and 20 to 30 hours of training in phone counseling. In return, you'll be asked for a commitment, such as working two 4-hour shifts a week for six months.

- Contact the United Way Homelessness Prevention Helpline in S.F., (415) 772-7390; the Contra County Homeless Hotline, (510) 646-1212; or your county's Homeless Coalition (see p. 81). (*Note:* Crisis hotlines also offer support and referrals to people in danger of becoming homeless; see p. 93).

ADOPT A FAMILY

Background. In this case, "adopting" can mean many different things, from helping out financially…to providing short-term help around the holidays…to becoming part of a family's life.

- "Adoption programs are a good way to contribute money, but in a personal way," says Carol Schick, a volunteer with the Family to Family Sharing program in San Mateo. "We 'adopt' a family every year at the holidays. First I ask the family what they want for Christmas—usually it's food and gifts for the children. My kids and I do the shopping together. Then our whole family goes to deliver the things, and we spend a couple of hours visiting."

Getting Started. Adoption programs are run by various organizations—shelters, transitional housing facilities, churches, etc.—and serve both homeless families and those in danger of becoming homeless. For info and referral, call local homeless organizations, your county Homeless Coalition (see p. 81), or a Volunteer Center (see p. 129).

HELP BUILD HOMES WITH ❂
HABITAT FOR HUMANITY

Background. Habitat for Humanity helps low-income people own their own homes. "We provide volunteers to build the house and arrange for an interest-free mortgage," says Chris Becker, a Habitat coordinator. "And each family is required to put in 500 hours in 'sweat equity.' " Most materials are donated as well.

- Volunteers help build or assist in planning. You don't have to know anything about construction. "While volunteers with experience are always needed, most Habitat workers are 'unskilled,' " says Tom O'Mahoney, a crew supervisor. "Tasks are broken down so that everyone who shows up at the site can help."

Getting Started. Start by attending a brief orientation. After that, you can just show up at the site. If you'd like to work in the office or serve on a committee, you can do anything from making a few phone calls to organizing a major fundraising effort.

• To find the nearest orientation meeting, call Habitat for Humanity's regional office, (510) 286-8960, or any local office: San Francisco, (415) 750-4780; Marin, (415) 721-4112; Peninsula, (415) 324-2266; San Jose, (408) 294-6464; East Bay, (510) 251-6304; Mt. Diablo, (510) 933-1296; Sonoma, (707) 578-7707.

☆   ☆   ☆

WORK WITH CHRISTMAS IN APRIL ✪

Background. There are many elderly and low-income people who have homes, but can't afford to keep them up. Some even live with safety hazards like rotting floors and bad electrical wiring. Christmas in April is an organization that helps people make repairs on their homes. They use volunteers for the work—most of which is done one day a year, on the last Saturday in April. How you can help:

• *Join a work crew.* You'll be assigned to a repair site. No construction skills are needed; the house captain will show you what to do.

• *Become a "house captain."* This is a good job if you can commit more time and you're good at organizing. You'll plan a job and help recruit people to work. "I oversaw a job we did for a 93-year-old woman living in a mobile home," says a volunteer in Sunnyvale. "I met with her a few times in advance, so I knew she needed to have her steps rebuilt and get the grease cleaned out of the fan over her stove. She hadn't been able to use it for a long time...she was *really* thrilled."

• *Help with fundraising, etc.* People are needed year-round to get materials donated, raise money, and help with publicity.

Getting Started. On-site work is a one-day commitment. After you register, you'll receive all pertinent information in the mail (what you'll be doing, when to be there, how to dress, etc.), then you can just show up. Becoming a House Captain is a bigger commitment. You'll need to meet with the homeowner, then plan the project.

• Call your local Christmas in April affiliate: Berkeley/Albany, c/o Interdependent Elders Network, (510) 644-8978; Castro Valley, (510) 581-5447; Oakland, (510) 451-4346; West Contra Costa, c/o Richmond Chamber of Commerce, (510) 234-3512; Marin, (415) 708-2366; Mid-Peninsula, (415) 361-4920; San Francisco, (415) 905-1611; South Bay, (408) 450-2227.

☆ ☆ ☆

RESOURCES

Homeless Coalitions. These organizations support agencies that provide services to homeless people. They exist in most Bay Area counties and can refer you to shelters and other programs that need help:

• Alameda County: Emergency Services Network, (510) 451-3138

• Contra Costa County: Association of Homeless & Housing Service Providers, c/o Shelter Inc., (510) 827-3598, ext. 106

• Marin County: Marin Countywide Homeless Connection, (415) 454-3234

• Napa County: Homeless Coalition, (707) 253-6103

• San Francisco County: San Francisco Council on Homelessness, (415) 357-4670

• San Mateo County: The Volunteer Center of San Mateo, (415) 342-0801

• Santa Clara County: Help House the Homeless, (408) 298-6401

• Solano County: Coalition Against Homelessness, (707) 427-8466

• Sonoma County: Sonoma County Task Force on the Homeless, (707) 527-2693

SUPPORT LOCAL ARTS AND CULTURE

In 1994, volunteers at the Oakland Museum gave tours to more than 55,000 visitors and organized a rummage sale that grossed over $450,000 for exhibits and events.

Y ou might not consider things like museums, movies, and art galleries "essential" community services. But imagine what life would be like without them.

Of course, you may already support the arts by buying tickets. But ticket sales are rarely enough to support arts groups. They depend on volunteers who appreciate what they're doing—and want to be a part of it.

DID YOU KNOW

• The Peninsula Civic Light Opera in San Mateo entertains about 30,000 people a year in 30 performances. Four hundred volunteers, who do everything from ushering to performing to building sets, make it possible.

• The Bay Area Book Festival now attracts more than 25,000 people a year—which makes it the largest book fair on the West Coast. It's put on by the San Francisco Bay Area Book Council, with four staff people...and over 400 volunteers.

• Several times a year, more than 1,000 volunteers pitch in to keep Bay Area public television and radio stations on the air. By answering phones during pledge drives, they help stations raise over 50% of their annual budgets.

• "Our volunteers use the arts to introduce people to other cultures," says Elena Serrano with La Pena Cultural Center in Berkeley. "They play an important role in preserving traditions and giving cultural groups a stronger sense of identity."

• "The more help an arts group gets, the more they can focus on being creative and polishing what they do," explains a community theater director. "Volunteers also allow us to keep ticket prices down and offer free performances at schools."

What You Can Do

WORK AT A MUSEUM ✪

Background. There's a wonderful variety of museums in the Bay Area—from the internationally renowned Museum of Modern Art to small specialty museums like S.F.'s Cartoon Art Museum and Marin's Native American Museum. All of them (*especially* the small ones) depend on volunteers. A few jobs to consider:

- *Staff the welcome desk.* "This is a good job for warm people who enjoy interacting with the public," says Phoebe Feinman with the Jewish Museum in San Francisco. "You'll greet visitors as they come in, keep an eye out for security, and maybe help in the museum shop."

- *Help curators.* This can mean researching the background of artwork or helping to organize and display it. One example: When a collector donated 5,000 opera, ballet, and theater programs to the San Francisco Performing Arts Library & Museum, Christine Smith volunteered to organize them. "I love history and the performing arts," she says, "so for me, the museum research room is the most wonderful environment. I once found a fan from 1860 that belonged to Lola Montez, a singer who had an affair with Franz Liszt. Sometimes I come out of there and it's a little shocking to be back in the 1990s."

- *Work behind the scenes.* Museums need help with a lot of different things—from getting out newsletters to maintaining galleries. "I do whatever's needed," says Keith Lewis, an artist and volunteer at the Cartoon Art Museum. "When we change shows, I go through and patch up holes in the walls and paint. Soon I'll be decorating the children's room. I'm going to make the heating duct look like a big worm."

- *Become a docent.* Docents take extensive courses and become experts on a museum's collections and exhibits—then lead tours for visitors, often schoolchildren. This involves a long-term commitment. At the Oakland Museum, for example, docents take college-level courses once a week for about a year, then volunteer twice a month for two years. Some museums charge a visitor's fee to offset the expense of the classes.

Getting Started. Each museum volunteer program is different. Most have short-term projects as well as a chance for a long-term commitment. Large museums are more formal and structured. In small museums, jobs tend to be less defined and volunteers wear a number of hats. For more information, look in the yellow pages under Museums. Call and ask for the Volunteer Coordinator.

☆　☆　☆

WORK IN A GALLERY

Background. This is a great way to support local artists and make sure that a wide range of art is available for public viewing. Nonprofit galleries, which specialize in art that isn't necessarily commercial, depend on volunteers to stay open. But even the fanciest galleries use volunteers in some roles.

• Most galleries need "sitters"—people who can be there for a few hours to answer questions and make visitors feel comfortable. They also need help hanging new shows, and help serving food and drinks at openings.

Getting Started. "Picking a gallery to work with is a very personal thing," says Heather Snider with Vision Gallery in S.F. "All galleries are different—from the people who run them to the kinds of art they show. So before you volunteer, you need to go there. Get a sense of the people, see if you like their approach and their taste in art."

• You'll find a complete list of galleries in the *San Francisco and Bay Area Gallery Guide* (available free at most fine art galleries). Galleries are also listed in the Pink Section of the *Sunday Examiner and Chronicle*.

☆　☆　☆

SUPPORT A PERFORMING ARTS GROUP ✪

Background. There are 250 community theater groups in the Bay Area and hundreds of other groups—dance companies, musical groups, puppet shows, circuses, etc. They'd love to have your help:

• *Assist with costumes or makeup.* "We buy the materials, and volunteers do all the sewing," says Marsha Schneider of the Rainbow Theater in Milpitas. If you can't sew, you can hunt for accessories, organize costumes, or help actors with makeup before shows. Some groups, like Make-a-Circus, may need volunteers to *design* costumes as well.

- *Help create sets.* This might mean painting, building, hanging backdrops and lights, or hunting for small props. Experience in set design or carpentry is appreciated, but usually not necessary.

- *Do fundraising and publicity.* "A lot of legwork needs to be done when you put on a performance," says Alison Schwarz, former manager of a Palo Alto dance company. "You may want to get businesses to advertise in the program. Someone has to put together press kits, call local media, and put up posters in local merchants' windows. Those things help make the show a success."

- *Volunteer at performances.* Performance groups need ushers, coat-checkers and people to stand at exit doors. "I can't afford to buy tickets for everything I want to see...so I usher five or six performances a month," says one volunteer. "It's a wonderful opportunity, but you have to take it seriously and follow through on your assignment or you won't be asked back."

Getting Started. Call a group for information and leave your name on their volunteer list. They'll contact you when they've got a project.

- *To find amateur and semi-professional theater companies:* Look under Stage Theater in the yellow pages; go through the Pink Section of the *Sunday Examiner and Chronicle*; call the theater departments of local colleges and universities; or call Theater Bay Area in San Francisco, (415) 957-1557. They publish *Call Board*, a magazine that lists volunteer needs (as well as auditions and performances) and can also refer you to a group over the phone.

- *To usher at large theaters:* Call the box office; let them know you want to volunteer for performances. The House Manager will call you back and make arrangements.

- *To find local dance companies:* Your best bet is to call the dance departments of local colleges and universities.

- *If you want to join the circus:* Call Make-a-Circus in San Francisco: (415) 242-1414.

HELP PUT ON THE S.F. BAY AREA BOOK FESTIVAL ⊙

Background. This annual two-day event in November promotes literacy and benefits the Bay Area's independent bookstores and publishers. It's already the biggest book festival on the West Coast... and it's getting bigger every year. Volunteers are needed to:

- *Help with planning and publicity.* Depending on how much time you put in, you can have a big impact on the festival. You can get involved with planning and see your ideas for author readings, panel discussions, workshops, etc., come to life. Or help with publicity by distributing posters to bookstores, answering phones, etc.

- *Work at the Festival.* During the event, volunteers escort authors, give out programs, sell book bags, and so on. "Most volunteers are people who'd come to the festival anyway," says Kathleen Copus with the S.F. Book Council. "About half the people are involved in publishing...or would like to be."

Getting Started. Planning committees begin meeting in April, but work more as the event nears. Festival volunteers attend an orientation meeting a couple months in advance, then sign up for one or more three-hour shifts. For info, call the San Francisco Bay Area Book Council, (415) 908-2833.

☆　☆　☆

HELP AT A FILM FESTIVAL ⊙

Background. Film festivals are an important part of the Bay Area cultural scene: They bring us documentaries and independent films we wouldn't see otherwise, and they provide a venue for local independent filmmakers. Here are a few ways you can support them:

- *Help with hospitality.* Most film festivals host at least two receptions—for opening night, for directors, or for celebrities. Volunteers greet guests, help set up and clean up, decorate, and serve food and drinks.

- *Work in the box office.* You'll sell tickets, keep track of reserve tickets, etc.

- *Keep things running smoothly.* Volunteers make sure people get to the right screening, take tickets, hand out film evaluation forms, answer questions, and so on.

Getting Started. Call a festival that interests you and see what they need. If possible, call two months in advance. Several to try: Asian American (March), (415) 863-0814; Black Filmworks (April), (510) 465-0804; S.F. International (April/May), (415) 929-5000; Gay & Lesbian (June), (415) 703-8650; Jewish (July/Aug), (415) 621-0556; Latino (Sept), (415) 553-8135; Mill Valley (Oct), (415) 383-5256; American Indian (Nov), (415) 554-0525.

• For general info, call the Film Arts Foundation, (415) 552-8760, or the Pacific Film Archive, (510) 642-1412 (they also have a year-round volunteer program).

☆　☆　☆

SUPPORT PUBLIC BROADCASTING ◌

Background. Public TV and radio stations rely on volunteers—and the money that volunteers help raise during membership drives and other events. How you can help:

• *Answer calls during membership pledge drives.* Pledge drives last 7 to 10 days, throughout broadcast hours. (Volunteers are especially needed during the day.) The schedule is divided into 3- to 5-hour shifts. "It's work, but it's fun too," says Susan Peterson, a volunteer. "The phones are busy during pledge breaks, but in between you chat with the other volunteers, have refreshments, and get a tour of the station."

• *Help with events.* KQED, for example, holds several special events a year—from food festivals to lectures. "There are always large mailings to get out beforehand," says Kathy Sato, the Volunteer Coordinator. "On the day of the event, we need people to help with food, take tickets, clean up...a bit of everything."

• *Work in the office.* A station's volunteer office may be able to place you in various departments, depending on your interests. "It's a chance to see how a public station operates," says Sato.

Getting Started. Call one of these stations and ask for the Volunteer Coordinator. KQED-TV and radio, S.F., (415) 553-2153; KALW radio, S.F., (415) 695-5740; KRCB-TV and radio, North Bay, (707) 585-8522; KPFA radio, Berkeley, (510) 848-6767; KALX radio, U.C. Berkeley, (510) 642-1111; KCSM-TV and radio, College of San Mateo, (415) 574-6586.

HELP KEEP OUR COMMUNITY HEALTHY

Using about 50% volunteer labor, the Irwin Memorial Blood Bank collects enough blood each year to supply 43 Bay Area hospitals and 10,000 patients who need regular transfusions to live.

Health care is one of the hottest issues of the 1990s—and it should be. Protecting people's health is a basic responsibility in any society. If this is one of *your* major concerns, then there's plenty you can do as a volunteer—from providing free medical care to teaching or taking Red Cross classes.

DID YOU KNOW

• In 1996, the Berkeley Free Clinic provided free health services to more than 4,300 clients. About 95% of the staff are volunteers.

• In 1996, Crisis Support Services of Alameda County handled over 48,000 hotline calls. The people who took the calls (and saved the lives of 50 callers) were all volunteers.

• Every year, 150,000 people in the Bay Area take American Red Cross courses in CPR and other health-related subjects. The 4,000 teachers are volunteers.

• In the San Francisco branch alone, volunteers with the American Lung Association give away nearly 800,000 health education brochures a year on such topics as smoking and nutrition.

• In 1996, volunteers at Merrithew Hospital in Martinez put in over 45,000 hours of work.

• At Oakland Children's Hospital, volunteers spend 2,000 hours a month with young patients at their bedsides or in the playroom. "When there are twenty kids in the playroom, some with IVs, some in beds, some in wheelchairs, two staff people can't handle them," says coordinator Laura Bergang. "Without volunteers, we sometimes wouldn't be able to open the playroom at all."

What You Can Do

WORK IN A HOSPITAL ⊙

Background. All hospitals—whether state-funded, nonprofit, or private—rely on volunteers. Each hospital volunteer program is a little different, but these are some of the jobs generally available:

• *Visit with adult patients.* Many patients don't have visitors. "We sit with them and talk for a while," says Jim Atherton, a volunteer with Kaiser in Hayward. "Sometimes we read aloud, play cards, help them write letters. It's important for people to have that contact. It seems to help them get better faster."

• *Spend time with young patients.* You might visit a child's bedside, work with children in a large playroom, or assist a teacher in a hospital school. "As soon as we get off the elevator, the kids see our blue volunteer shirts and come running," says Bill Raha, who volunteers with his wife, Nancy, at Oakland Children's Hospital. "Sometimes you forget that they're even sick. Other times it's hard; some kids aren't going to make it. But at least you can say you did something to make their life more enjoyable."

• *Hold babies in the nursery.* "Babies in the hospital need human contact, not just medical care, to get healthy," explains Barbara Olsen, a volunteer "cuddler" at Berkeley's Alta Bates. "Mostly, I hold babies who are hurting or don't get visited often. Some are withdrawing from drugs, some are abandoned. The babies are every race, every weight...It's a wonderful job."

• *Be a liaison in surgery and emergency rooms.* You tell doctors who's waiting for news (so they'll know who to talk to), and tell families when a patient is in the recovery room. Explains one volunteer: "You can do a lot to comfort people...but you need to be able to work well under pressure."

• *Work in the health education center.* Most hospitals have a place where people can find information on their illness or surgery. Volunteers keep resources organized and mail materials out or take them to patients' rooms.

• *Make baby blankets.* If you enjoy knitting or crocheting, you can volunteer to make receiving blankets, caps, and booties for newborns. "We like to send mothers home with something nice for their babies, especially mothers who can't buy those things," says Fredette Pardini with Merrithew Memorial Hospital in Martinez. Some hospitals have formal knitting programs with patterns and guidelines. Others don't, but will happily take donated items.

Getting Started. Hospitals and health-care centers are listed in the yellow pages under Hospitals. Most hold regular volunteer orientation sessions. This is a good way to get an overview of available jobs, including the training and commitment involved. Be prepared to go through a health screening process as well, which usually includes a TB test and various vaccines. (Some hospitals cover the expense, others don't.)

☆　☆　☆

FIGHT A DEADLY DISEASE ◐

Background. Groups like the American Heart Association and Breast Cancer Action help combat major illnesses. Through a local chapter, you can raise money for research, educate the public, and provide special services for patients.

• "Even the most routine jobs are important. I answer the phone at the American Cancer Society once a week for two or three hours," says Lena Lindgren. "I take down information about what the person is interested in—the kind of cancer, when it was diagnosed, etc.—and then I send brochures. People are grateful that someone is there to answer their questions."

Getting Started. Decide what disease you want to work on, then call groups working in that area and see what kind of help they need. Look for local groups in the yellow pages under Social Service Organizations, or ask a doctor for a referral.

• Here are a few of the larger health organizations that work on a particular health problem; call them for referral to a local chapter: American Diabetes Association, (800) 828-8293; American Lung Association, (800) 586-4872; National Multiple Sclerosis Society, (800) FIGHT-MS; American Cancer Society, (800) 227-2345; American Heart Association, (800) 242-8721; Breast Cancer Action Network, (415) 243-9301.

WORK IN A FREE CLINIC ✪

Background. Free clinics offer basic medical care and anonymous HIV testing as a community service. Most of their clients have little money and no health insurance. If you just want to volunteer for a short time each week, you could work at the front desk—checking in patients, answering questions, and making appointments. If you want to get more involved, you can be trained to perform basic medical procedures.

Getting Started. There are 13 free clinics in the Bay Area covering general health and several others that specialize in one area, such as ear, nose, and throat. To find a free clinic, look in the Community Service section of the yellow pages under Health Care. Or call one clinic and ask for a list of the others. (*Note*: Marin County has no free clinics, but its low-cost clinics need volunteers.)

GIVE BLOOD OR WORK IN A BLOOD BANK ✪

Background. Hospitals and clinics desperately need blood for surgeries and transfusions, but only about 5% of eligible people in the Bay Area donate. Volunteers are needed to recruit people, to help donors register, to assist medical staff, etc.

• "Some people are a little nervous; maybe they've never given blood before," says Juanita Guisto, a blood bank volunteer. "We help them calm down. Afterward, we observe them to be sure they don't feel faint. Most of the donors are a delight. They're there to give blood for others. It's a pleasure to take care of them."

Getting Started. When you volunteer, you'll go through a two-hour orientation, then choose a job. Most people work a two- to four-hour shift, once a week or twice a month. But blood banks are happy to have whatever time you can give.

• You might also consider donating blood—especially if you have a rare blood type. It typically takes less than an hour.

• In the San Jose area, call the American Red Cross, Northern California Blood Services, Office of Volunteers, (408) 577-2032. They'll refer you to the nearest blood bank. Elsewhere, call Bay Area Blood Centers, (800) 864-4835.

TAKE, OR TEACH, A RED CROSS CLASS ✪

Background. In the Bay Area, the American Red Cross offers 200 classes a month—taught by volunteer instructors—on subjects ranging from CPR to avoiding back injury.

- "Learning CPR and first aid could save the life of someone you know, and it also makes for a safer community," says Myra Green, a Red Cross volunteer coordinator. "It means more people can help if a disaster or accident occurs."

Getting Started. To take a class, call the American Red Cross, (800) 520-5433, and get the schedule for your area. To be an instructor, you'll need to be proficient in what you're teaching, then take two instructor classes. You can usually teach as often as you like.

☆   ☆   ☆

WORK IN A HOSPICE

Background. Hospices offer support to terminally ill people—either in their own home or in a residential facility. They train volunteers to make patients and families as comfortable as possible—by visiting, spending time with kids, helping with laundry, etc.

- "When someone is dying, families often don't know what to do. The presence of a hospice worker—someone who has experience with the situation—helps them communicate and express their needs," says Laura Besecker of Mission Hospice in Burlingame. "It's very rewarding to support a family at a time when they need it so much."

Getting Started. To work directly with patients and families, you'll need to take a 25-hour course—usually 2 1/2 hours a week for 10 weeks. Ideally, you'd then be available four hours a week, for a year. But hospices are flexible. If you can only work occasionally, you can do errands for the hospice—like picking up prescriptions—without training.

- To find local hospices, call the California State Hospice Association, (916) 441-3770. Or look in the yellow pages under Hospices.

ANSWER A CRISIS HOTLINE

Background. There are nine crisis/suicide-prevention hotlines in the Bay Area. All are answered by trained volunteers.

- "Most people imagine we handle one desperate rescue after another," says Glen Gold, a former volunteer. "The truth is, only about 3% of callers are actively trying to commit suicide. About a third are ordinary people in crisis, and the rest are repeat callers whose daily lives are a perpetual struggle. Having someone they can reach out to is crucial."

Getting Started. Answering a crisis hotline isn't for everyone—organizations only accept people who are "emotionally mature, non-judgmental and able to cope well with stress." If accepted, you'll take about 12 hours of classes and go through about 60 hours of on-the-job training. Most programs ask for a one-year commitment, which includes training time.

- For more info, call directory assistance and ask for the nearest crisis hotline. If possible, get the administration number.

HELP AT A DRUG OR ALCOHOL REHAB PROGRAM

Background. Substance-abuse programs help people with addictions rebuild their lives. Most offer counseling, peer support, information, etc. Volunteers do a number of things—from working in the office, to watching children while parents attend meetings, to accompanying people to doctor appointments.

- "Part of recovery is dealing with unresolved problems," says Linda Palmer, a program coordinator. "So, as a volunteer, you might be helping people get their children or job back, or get needed medical care. It's rewarding to work with people who are making positive changes in their lives."

Getting Started. Commitment levels vary. Most programs are happy to have whatever time you can give. To find a rehab program near you, look in the Community Service section of the yellow pages under Alcohol and Drug Abuse.

TAKE CARE
OF OUR PARKS

The San Francisco Bay Area has more than 225,000
acres of parkland, with 3,000 to 4,000 miles of trails.

I f you like being outdoors, you probably appreciate the Bay
Area's great parks...and you know how much they mean to
our communities.

But you may not realize that, behind the scenes, park departments are strapped for cash. Many are having a hard time supplying
basic services...and even keeping up with maintenance.

Fortunately, park lovers are stepping in to give them a hand—
painting swings, planting flowers, clearing trails, and much more.
It's a great way to combine outdoor time with community service.

DID YOU KNOW

• When Proposition 13 passed in 1978, California cities and
counties lost much of the tax money that traditionally went to
maintain parks and other public outdoor areas.

• "Over the years, our parks have deteriorated," says Joel Wither-
ell, Berkeley Parks Manager. "We're doing just the minimum.
There's usually enough money to mow the lawn once in a while,
but not enough to put flowers in the flower beds or replace an irri-
gation system that's more than thirty years old."

• Hundreds of neighborhood "Friends of the Park" groups now
help care for local parks. In San Rafael, for example, Friends of
Pickleweed Park planted trees, installed play structures, painted a
mural, and more.

• Lots of other groups are helping, too. In Santa Rosa, for example, a class from a high school for troubled teenagers adopted a
creek in a community park. "We had no way of maintaining the
trail along the stream until the students pitched in," says a city official. "The kids' work saves the city money and provides better recreation for everyone."

What You Can Do

JOIN A LOCAL PARK GROUP ✪

Background. Neighborhood "Friends of the Park" groups have become very important, because they do work that city park systems can't afford. Even if you've never heard of them, there may be a group caring for a park near your home.

• As a volunteer, you can just show up to work with the group in the park once in a while, volunteer to contact interested neighbors, or oversee a whole project. Many groups organize weekend workdays for people to work together planting, weeding, cleaning, etc. "This is a great way to meet people in your area," says Rita Shue with the Hayward park and rec office. "Everyone cares about the park, so you have something in common."

• Working with city government, a park group can accomplish larger projects as well. "We put in a 'tot lot' for kids, disabled-access pathways and eighteen new trees," says Bill Lipsky with Friends of Willard Park in Berkeley. "It makes our park much more of a community gathering place."

Getting Started. Find out if your park has a "Friends of the Park" group by calling the city Parks Manager or Volunteer Manager (see p. 128). If there is a group, call to find out what they're working on. If there's not a group, you may want to form one. Call your local Volunteer Center (see p. 129) for more information.

☆　☆　☆

GET AN ADOPT-A-PARK GRANT

Background. In many cities, your Friends of the Park group or Parks Manager can get you an adopt-a-park grant. This covers the cost of materials for doing small projects in your neighborhood park—such as replacing dead flowers in flower beds or keeping park benches graffiti-free.

Getting Started. Call your city Parks Manager or local Friends of the Park group and ask them to help you work out the details.

SUPPORT A COMMUNITY GARDEN ✪

Background. If you love to garden but don't have a place to do it... want to turn a trash-strewn vacant lot into something beautiful... or just want to spend time with neighbors, a community garden could be the ideal place for you to get involved. What you can do:

• *Work your own garden plot, or help someone else.* Most community gardens are divided into plots. You can cultivate a plot of your own (there's often a waiting list) or share one. The garden coordinator can probably match you with a plot owner who wants help. For example, some seniors have plots, but need help with heavy work. It's a great way to learn from an experienced gardener.

• *Start a new garden.* This is a big job, but community garden organizations like San Francisco Urban Gardeners (SLUG) can lead you through the process. "You'll be creating something green and beautiful," says Brain Lease of SLUG. "But it's more than that. It's about neighbors working side by side, making decisions together, learning together."

Getting Started. Call these groups for info or referral: East Bay Urban Gardeners, (510) 834-5342; San Francisco League of Urban Gardeners, (415) 285-7584; East Palo Alto Historical and Agricultural Society, (415) 329-0294; Community Garden Program, City of San Jose Streets and Parks Department, (408) 277-2575.

• Special garden projects that also need volunteers: The Garden Project, San Bruno County Jail, (415) 243-8558; SMCO Probation garden project, Hillcrest Juvenile Hall, (650) 312-8826; Homeless Garden Project, Santa Cruz, (408) 426-3609.

☆　☆　☆

MAINTAIN TRAILS AND OPEN SPACES ✪

Background. Bay Area regional, state, and national parks contain thousands of miles of trails—all of which need regular maintenance to be safe, and to remain open. Unfortunately, park budgets can't always cover the cost. How you can help:

• *Participate in workday events.* At a regular time each week or month, volunteers work in crews to pick up litter, clear brush, plant trees, etc. You can usually just show up. Bring lunch, a pair of work gloves, and good work shoes...and enjoy a day outdoors.

- *Patrol trails.* This is a great way to hike and help at the same time. "We depend on volunteers to hike the smaller trails that we don't get to as often," says Kathleen Fusek of the East Bay Regional Park District. "They watch for trouble spots—fallen trees, storm erosion, that kind of thing. Then they report back, and we send a crew to fix the problem."

- *Assist park rangers.* If you can volunteer once or twice a month on an ongoing basis, you can work alongside rangers building and restoring trails. It's great exercise and an excellent chance to learn something about native plants and ecosystems.

- *Lead work crews.* Most parks could use even more volunteers if they had more people to oversee projects. "We need people to help plan workdays," says a ranger at Golden Gate National Recreation Area, "then come out and supervise volunteers." If you've helped fix trails, this is a logical next step.

Getting Started. Call your regional park district or a nearby state or national park (see p. 99), and ask about volunteer opportunities. They can send you a list of scheduled workdays and tell you more about other jobs. (*Note:* You can patrol a trail and report problems any time you hike. If you want to go where you're most needed, check with a ranger before you set out.)

WORK IN A PARK VISITOR CENTER

Background. Volunteers staff most regional, state, and national park visitor centers and information kiosks. "Most of the time it's just a matter of giving directions and answering simple questions," says Terry Kreidler, a volunteer coordinator with GGNRA. "In fact, the most common question is 'where's the bathroom?' "

- "If you like dealing with the public, it's a lot of fun," she adds. "You give people the information they need to get out and enjoy the park and free up rangers to do other important things."

Getting Started. Visitor center volunteers are trained in "people contact" and given a short course on the park's history and resources (about four hours). Programs vary. Most ask that, once trained, you commit to working a four-hour shift once a week for several months.

- For more info, call your regional park district, or a nearby state or national park (see p. 99).

☆　☆　☆

DO ADMINISTRATIVE WORK ✪

Background. City park and rec departments are inundated with paperwork several times a year, as people register for tennis lessons, swim classes, and day camps. Most need help with data entry, filing, and answering the phone.

- "Phone calls and forms coming in the mail are usually more than the regular clerical staff can handle," explains Joan Carrico, formerly with the Milpitas park and rec department. "It might not be as exciting as being outdoors, but it's vital to the park department."

Getting Started. This work doesn't involve a long-term commitment. If you can come in a few times a year when the work piles up, you'll help a lot. Call your park department for more info.

☆　☆　☆

BECOME A PARK DOCENT

Background. Park docents are especially dedicated volunteers who learn about a park and its ecosystems, then lead nature hikes and tours, and give presentations.

- "In some programs, docents receive as much training as entry level rangers," says Greg Archibald of the GGNRA. "They learn biology, cultural history, and local environmental issues. They're trained in public speaking skills, group dynamics and taught how to talk to different age groups. It's a great learning opportunity."

Getting Started. Most docent programs involve a minimum of 40 hours for training and ask for a long-term commitment, such as two tours a month for a year. Some charge a small fee as well, to offset the cost of training. Call your regional park district or a nearby state or national park (see p. 99) for information.

RESOURCES

Regional Park Districts. Ask for the Volunteer Coordinator:

- ❖ East Bay Regional Park District, Alameda and Contra Costa counties, (510) 635-0135, ext. 2515
- ❖ Marin County Open Spaces District, (415) 499-3778
- ❖ Sonoma County Regional Park District—call Spring Lake Park, (707) 539-8092
- ❖ San Mateo County Parks, (415) 363-4020
- ❖ Santa Clara County Parks and Rec Dept., (408) 358-3741, ext. 163
- ❖ Solano County Regional Parks, (707) 421-7925
- ❖ Napa County—Skyline Wilderness Park is run by a nonprofit that needs volunteers, (707) 252-0481

State Parks. To volunteer in state parks, call any park directly or call your State Park District office for a referral.

- ❖ Bay Area District—San Francisco, San Mateo, and Contra Costa counties, (415) 330-6300
- ❖ Marin District, (415) 456-1286
- ❖ Silverado District in Sonoma, (707) 938-1519
- ❖ Russian River/Mendocino District, (707) 865-2391
- ❖ Santa Cruz District, (408) 429-2850
- ❖ For state parks in Alameda County, call the East Bay Regional Park District, (510) 635-0138, ext. 2515

Golden Gate National Recreation Area. Call for a current list of ongoing volunteer opportunities and work events: (415) 556-3535.

Green City Volunteer Network. They offer a free quarterly calendar that lists volunteer opportunities and events in parks, community gardens, and environmental groups. They may also be able to refer you to smaller neighborhood groups. Call (415) 285-6556.

SUPPORT LIBRARIES AND LITERACY

Libraries are among the Bay Area's most frequently used public facilities. An estimated 78% of the population uses them each year.

T he public library is an amazing community resource. You can find practically any kind of information there. Looking for work? There's data on local companies. Concerned about your kids? There are books on parenting. Want to volunteer? They have lists of nonprofits.

Libraries also provide valuable people-to-people services. In a Richmond library, for example, a lawyer gives free legal advice twice a month; the Berkeley Public Library has free Internet classes; and the San Francisco Public Library has magic shows for kids.

Unfortunately, libraries are struggling financially. Severe budget cuts have forced many to reduce hours and staff, even eliminate programs. They need our help.

DID YOU KNOW

• California libraries are currently going through their worst budget crisis since Prop. 13 passed in 1978. In 1993-1994, for example, the Alameda County library system lost about 50% of its funding—and at one point had to close some branches completely.

• Bay Area residents help local libraries make up for these losses with more than half a million hours of volunteer work a year.

• In the Contra Costa County system, for example, volunteers contribute over 35,000 hours a year. "Without them, we couldn't offer homework help or literacy programs," says Director Anne Cain. "And there'd be no special workshops, like Grandparents and Books, where volunteers teach seniors how to pick books for kids."

• Most people get involved with libraries through Friends of the Library (FOL) groups. These provide essential support by raising money, running special programs, and recruiting volunteers.

• The work of FOL volunteers preserves an important part of American life. To quote the *San Francisco Chronicle*: "Libraries remain the nation's most democratic institution. There is no tradition more deserving of honor and support."

What You Can Do

WORK IN A LIBRARY ✪

Background. When people in the community help keep their library running, it means librarians can focus on things like assisting people with research or improving programs and services. What volunteers can do:

• *Maintain books.* "There are always books that need a little minor mending, a little gluing," says Helen Dunbar of the Alameda County Library. "And books need to be weeded out of the collection periodically, so they can be prepared for a book sale or for discard." Books have to be processed when they're first purchased, too.

• *Staff the welcome desk.* If you enjoy talking to people, you can volunteer to sit at a library's information desk and answer basic questions about library cards, locations of books and periodicals, etc. This involves a short training session, and you'll probably need to commit to working a shift (a few hours) on a regular basis. "A library can be intimidating to people who've never been there before," says Patricia Coyle, a volunteer at the S.F. Public Library. "So it's nice if there's a friendly face to greet them."

• *Support an ongoing program.* Most libraries have plenty of volunteer-driven activities going on that need help—lectures, author appearances, reading programs for kids, etc.

• *Take on a special project.* If you have special skills or knowledge you'd like to share, you can turn it into a special project. Libraries are always open to new ideas, especially if you're willing to do what it takes to make your idea come to life.

One Example: Businessman Gul Wadwani volunteered to improve the business reference files for a branch of the Alameda County Library. He scanned journals and papers for up-to-date information about local businesses, then organized it. "It's important to keep up with recent developments for people who are looking for employment," he explains. "It's very satisfying to me to be able to do this for the public."

Getting Started. Contact your local library or Friends of the Library (FOL) group for details.

HELP WITH LIBRARY BOOK SALES ✪

Background. Libraries rely on book sales to raise money for exhibits, new book purchases, and renovations. People are needed to pick up donated books, sort them, price them, and work on sale days. If you like books, this can be a lot of fun. You get to handle many old, interesting books—and you get first crack at picking out the ones you want for your own collection.

Getting Started. Book sales only happen occasionally, but the process of gathering and sorting books goes on year-round. Call your local library or FOL group to see when they need help.

☆ ☆ ☆

TALK TO KIDS ABOUT BOOKS ✪

Background. Many libraries make a special effort to get kids interested in reading. They train volunteers to read aloud in schools or present new books that students might not have heard of.

• "It's a way to reach non-reading students with the idea that books are fun and interesting," says Dominik Hutches, a volunteer with the Fremont Public Library. "You're taught to 'tell' a book—to make it something exciting for children to the point where they've *got* to check it out."

Getting Started. Call your local public library or FOL group, and ask if they have a "book talk" program.

☆ ☆ ☆

GET INVOLVED IN LIBRARY OUTREACH PROGRAMS ✪

Background. Sometimes libraries don't just wait for visitors. Through special programs, they get books to people who can't come in—people in nursing homes, hospitals, or prisons, or people who are homebound. As a volunteer, your visit may mean as much to people as the books you bring.

• Through a program called SOS (Senior Outreach Services), for example, Connie Gertsch and her two children bring books to nursing homes twice a month. "First we pick out books from the senior large-type section of the library," she says. "Then we take them to the home and go room to room with our cart asking residents if they'd like a book. Our regulars are always happy to see us. My kids usually bring something to show, so it's a visiting time, too."

Getting Started. Particulars—how often you go, how much time you spend visiting, etc.—will depend on the program. In some cases, you just deliver books, then pick them up. For more info, contact your library or FOL group; ask about outreach programs.

☆   ☆   ☆

TEACH SOMEONE HOW TO READ ✪

Background. Most literacy programs in the Bay Area are run through local libraries. They match volunteers with adults who can't read or have trouble reading. Sometimes tutors use software to teach, so students learn computer skills as well as reading skills. In general, literacy programs fall into two categories:

• *"Student-centered" programs*—for people who already have some reading skills. First you'll assess your student's strengths and weaknesses, then you'll create assignments based on what your student wants to learn, using practical sources—newspapers, magazines, grocery lists, food container labels, etc.

• *Beginner programs*—for people with few reading skills. You'll most likely use textbooks and workbooks provided by the program. You simply point to a picture, a letter, or a word, say it out loud, and repeat it.

• Literacy tutoring takes patience, but students' progress is often obvious from the beginning. "I tutor a woman who moved a lot when she was young, so she never got comfortable reading," says Bill Carney, a tutor in South San Francisco. "She'll bring in an article, and we'll go over it. We spend a lot of time talking about ideas, as well as words she's not familiar with. It's a process of rebuilding her self-confidence. After only a month, she felt able to read a menu in a restaurant for the first time. Before that, she wouldn't have even tried."

Getting Started. First, you'll be asked to take a tutoring workshop (3 to 15 hrs., depending on the program). Then you'll be matched with a student. The two of you can decide where and when to meet—the library, either person's home, wherever's convenient. Most programs ask you to commit to an amount of tutoring time, usually about 2 hours a week, for a few months to a year.

• For a referral, call your library, the Literacy Alliance, (408) 453-6711, or your volunteer center (see p. 129). You can also call the Bay Area Literacy Hotline, (800) 262-2123. (*Note:* They pass names to local programs once a month.)

• **Work/Study students** can teach young children to read in a program called America Reads. Ask your counselor for more info.

☆ ☆ ☆

TEACH ENGLISH AS A SECOND LANGUAGE

Background. There are many immigrants in the Bay Area who need to learn English—or get more comfortable using the English they know. English as a Second Language (ESL) or English for International Students (EIS) classes are offered in universities, community colleges, adult schools, cultural centers, nonprofits, and some libraries. Teachers need tutors to practice with students in class; formal tutoring programs match tutors and learners.

• People interested in other cultures often make the best ESL tutors. "You learn a lot about other parts of the world," explains Ida Daroza, an ESL volunteer. "You also end up explaining how things are done here in America. I feel like I'm involved in an intercultural exchange, as well as a tutor-student relationship."

• Some volunteers just talk to students and help them with pronunciation. This involves little or no training and can often be done on a drop-in basis. Other tutoring programs train volunteers, then match them with one student at a time and ask for a commitment to tutoring a certain number of hours a week.

Getting Started. To find ESL programs, ask at your local library, look in the Community Services section of the yellow pages under Immigrants and Refugees, call Literacy Alliance, (408) 453-6711, or contact a local university or college. (*Note:* Some adult schools and community colleges don't have formal volunteer programs, so volunteering with them may take time to set up. Leave your name and number with the ESL or EIS Coordinator and ask them to pass it to a teacher.)

REACH OUT TO PEOPLE WITH DISABILITIES

According to the American Disabilities Act, 18% to 20% of the American population has a mental or physical disability.

One of the hardest things about having a disability is the way it can isolate a person. It can be hard to participate in the community if, for example, it's a challenge just to go shopping or answer mail. A volunteer can make a big difference.

"It's all about access," explains one coordinator. "Volunteers can make it possible for someone with a disability to play on a sports team, take a class, learn to use special equipment...or just go out and have fun."

DID YOU KNOW

• The Special Olympics—which is almost entirely volunteer-run—gives over 6,000 people in the Bay Area who have disabilities the chance to be athletes. "Success on the playing field carries over to every other area of their life," says one volunteer.

• Through the Rose Resnick Lighthouse for the Blind and Visually Impaired, more than 80 "personal services" volunteers assist people with simple household chores.

• "The help really enhances their lives," explains Pam Spindler with Rose Resnick. "It means they don't always have to rely on friends and family—they can be more independent. When they get together with friends, they can do other things. They don't have to ask them to read their mail every time they visit."

• "When you work with people with special needs, you start to see the world differently," says Margo Roeckl, a volunteer white-water rafting guide who takes people with disabilities on wilderness trips. "You see people overcoming such enormous challenges, it changes your view of what abilities *are*—and your own limitations."

• If you're a *volunteer* with a disability, and you would like support with the process of volunteering, you can contact your local Volunteer Center (see p. 129).

WHAT YOU CAN DO

ASSIST SOMEONE IN THEIR HOME ✪

Background. A lot of everyday tasks, from answering mail to shopping for food, are challenging for people with disabilities. As a volunteer, you can help someone get things done, either occasionally or on a regular basis, and offer companionship, too.

Getting Started. The right program can match you with someone whose needs fit what you can offer. "For example, we have a client who is unable to speak due to a stroke," explains one coordinator. "A volunteer with computer skills helps him get into the Internet. It means he's able to continue contributing in his field as a scientist."

 • Call one of these groups for info or referral: Rose Resnick Lighthouse for the Blind or Visually Impaired, S.F., (415) 431-1481; Peninsula Center for the Blind and Visually Impaired, (415) 858-0202; Berkeley/Albany Interdependent Elders Network, (510) 644-8978; Senior Coastsiders, Half Moon Bay, (415) 726-9056.

☆   ☆   ☆

HELP OUT IN A SKILLS PROGRAM ✪

Background. There are dozens of programs in the Bay Area designed to help people with disabilities learn "self-care skills" (how to brush teeth, comb hair, etc.) or "living skills" (how to handle money, take public transportation, etc.).

 • "Volunteers give people a chance to practice these skills," says Mony Flores-Bauer of the Regional Center of the East Bay. "Working one-on-one, you might help someone register to vote, learn basic cooking skills...or go with them to the laundromat three or four times so they can get comfortable with the route."

Getting Started. This involves some on-the-job training. The time commitment depends on the program and the client's needs. Call for info or referral: Recreation Center for the Handicapped, S.F., (415) 665-4100; Community Vocational Enterprise, S.F., (415) 544-0424; Marin Assn. for Retarded Citizens, (415) 472-2373; California Autism Foundation, Richmond, (510) 758-0433; Growth Opportunities, Santa Rosa (707) 571-7637; Hope Rehabilitation Services, San Jose, (408) 748-2850. Or call your local Regional Center (see p. 111).

SUPPORT THE SPECIAL OLYMPICS ✪

Background. This national program gives people with developmental disabilities (e.g., mental retardation, autism, cerebral palsy) a chance to grow by developing physical skills, learning to work on a team with others, competing in sports tournaments, and winning ribbons and trophies. There are 30 different sports, played seasonally. Volunteer opportunities vary depending on the needs of local chapters.

• *Assist at games and tournaments.* "Event volunteers" help athletes get to their race or game on time and cheer them on from the sidelines. "The meets are a sight to see," says Linda Ledone with Special Olympics in Marin. "Hundreds of athletes in a big arena doing every kind of sport you can imagine...and loving it. Our regular volunteers wouldn't miss it for anything."

• *Coach a team.* Coaches and assistant coaches help athletes improve skills, sports knowledge, and self-esteem. "It's exciting to see people with a handicap really work at getting better," says Terry Kotter, a volunteer track coach. "They have as much heart as any athlete, they just weren't dealt the cards."

• *Do fund-raising or publicity.* Most Special Olympics programs hold fundraising events during the year to pay for uniforms, sports equipment, etc. People are needed to serve on committees and help at events.

Getting Started. Check the phone book for the Special Olympics chapter nearest you, or call the Northern California regional office in Pleasant Hill, (510) 944-8801, for a referral. Your local chapter can help you find something to match your schedule.

☆　☆　☆

HELP ON OUTINGS OR TRIPS ✪

Background. Several groups in the Bay Area arrange fun outings for people with disabilities. These trips range from picnics on Angel Island to cross-country ski weekends. As a volunteer, you can go on day outings and help prepare food, assist clients, etc., or if you really like sports and the outdoors, you can train to lead wilderness adventures.

• "Wilderness trips are an incredible experience for the people who go," says Margo Roeckl, a volunteer white-water rafting guide. "It's a real challenge for them, overcoming their limitations. It gives them an enormous feeling of accomplishment."

Getting Started. Volunteers on day outings get some on-the-job training, and the commitment is minimal. Call for info or referral: Bay Area Outreach and Recreation Program (BORP), Berkeley, (510) 849-4663; Rose Resnick Lighthouse for the Blind and Visually Impaired, S.F., (415) 431-1481; California Autism Foundation, Richmond (ask for the Volunteer Manager), (510) 758-0433; Growth Opportunities, Santa Rosa, (707) 571-7637; Hope Rehabilitation Services, San Jose, (408) 748-2850.

• Becoming an outdoor adventure *guide*, on the other hand, requires extensive training. You'll learn safety and rescue techniques and take courses in environmental awareness and disability sensitivity. Then you'll commit to guiding a certain number of trips. Contact Environmental Traveling Companions (ETC), S.F., (415) 474-7662.

☆ ☆ ☆

WORK IN SPORTS AND RECREATION PROGRAMS ◗

Background. Hundreds of people in the Bay Area with physical disabilities are active in adapted sports like "wheelchair basketball" and "power soccer" (played in power wheelchairs). They play in tournaments that draw teams from around the country. A large number of volunteers are needed to assist coaches, pick up visiting teams from the airport, keep score, referee, etc.

• "These are high-energy, exciting games," says Rick Spittler with Bay Area Outreach and Recreation Program (BORP). "My only advice to volunteers is that you come with an open mind and some humility. Expect to learn a lot, and have fun."

Getting Started. Start at whatever level of involvement is comfortable. You can help out just at tournaments or join a team as an assistant coach and be there for practices and other games. Volunteers are also needed to help in recreation programs that feature non-team sports.

• Call for info: BORP, Berkeley, (510) 849-4663; Recreation Center for the Handicapped, S.F., (415) 665-4100; San Jose Dept. of Therapeutic Services, (408) 267-0200. Or try city park and rec departments, YMCAs, YWCAs, Jewish Community Centers, and similar organizations. They often have such programs, too.

HELP OUT IN AN INDEPENDENT LIVING CENTER

Background. Independent Living Centers (ILCs) help people with disabilities find and adapt housing, get benefits, learn to use special equipment, etc.

• "Our goal is to help our consumers to become independent by overcoming obstacles," says Nancy Lara-Moscardini at the ILC in Marin. "More than anything, we need people to help us in the office. We have a lot of mailings going out to keep people up on laws that affect them and tell them about cuts in social security benefits. Volunteers help us keep current."

Getting Started. Call the ILC nearest you: Berkeley, (510) 841-4776; Hayward, (510) 881-5743; Martinez, (510) 229-9200; Marin, (415) 459-6245; San Francisco, (415) 863-0581; Belmont, (415) 595-0783; Santa Clara, (408) 985-1243; Capitola, (408) 462-8720; Salinas, (408) 757-2968; Santa Rosa, (707) 528-2745.

☆ ☆ ☆

RECORD BOOKS FOR THE BLIND

Background. Books on tape give people who are visually impaired a chance to experience literature and use educational materials they wouldn't otherwise have access to. You can help make tapes available by becoming a "reader."

• "Each recording session is an hour long," says Mayetta Behringer, a volunteer with Books Aloud in San Jose. "Your voice can't last much more than that. You come in at a scheduled time, sit in the sound-proof studio, and read into a microphone. We get wonderful notes and letters from people who are very grateful that the service exists."

Getting Started. Most programs ask readers to audition first. Some ask that you start as a "monitor," which means sitting outside the recording booth and following the text to make sure the reader doesn't skip words. After a few weeks you can take a voice test, and, if you pass, become a reader.

- Call Recording for the Blind, Palo Alto, (415) 493-3717, or Books Aloud (popular fiction), San Jose, (408) 277-4878.

☆ ☆ ☆

RAISE A GUIDE DOG PUPPY ◐

Background. For some people with disabilities, a dog can make a huge difference in their quality of life. Organizations that train guide dogs need volunteers to raise their puppies—usually from about 8 weeks to 15 months old—then give them back for training. This is a good way for animal lovers to volunteer—it takes a very special dog, raised in just the right way, to be a guide dog.

- "A dog raised in a home is friendlier and more stable than a dog raised in a kennel," explains Rachel Zuiderweg with Guide Dogs for the Blind in San Rafael. "The puppy needs to be exposed to a range of sights and noises, and volunteers can give them those experiences."

Getting Started. Organizations prefer that puppy-raisers have a fenced yard or access to a fenced area. They will pay for the dog's shots, but you pay for dog food and possibly veterinary care (both are usually tax deductible). The puppies need to be exposed to kids and other pets, so if you already have some in the family, all the better.

- For info, call Canine Companions, (800) 572-BARK, or Guide Dogs for the Blind, (415) 499-4000.

☆ ☆ ☆

BE A MENTOR TO A CHILD WITH A DISABILITY

Background. Some mentoring programs (see p. 33) match adult mentors with children who have physical, developmental, or emotional disabilities. These children need extra attention, especially if they're part of a large family or a single-parent household.

- "I meet with a seven-year-old boy who's autistic," says Leanne Lustica, a mentor in San Francisco. "He has a twin brother who's not autistic and can take part in more activities. My role is to be a special friend to Kevin, to take him out and do things *he* enjoys, like watching the birds at Stowe Lake in Golden Gate Park."

Getting Started. Mentoring involves a commitment—usually at least one year. It's important that if a child invests in a relationship, it won't disappear. The amount of time you spend with the child depends on the program.

• Big Brothers/Big Sisters, for example, asks for two to three hours, as a minimum, every other week. Call the San Francisco Chapter of Big Brothers/Big Sisters, (415) 693-7700.

• There are few formal mentoring programs for disabled children, but each county has a Family Resource Center, which provides information and emotional support to families with disabled kids. Call the center in your county for info or referral: Alameda, (510) 547-7322; Contra Costa, (510) 313-0999; Marin, (415) 499-3877; Monterey, (408) 424-2937; San Francisco, (415) 282-7494; San Mateo, (415) 344-6673; Santa Clara, (408) 727-5775; North Santa Cruz, (408) 464-0669; South Santa Cruz (408) 761-6082; Solano, (707) 552-9845; Sonoma/Napa, (707) 586-3314.

☆ ☆ ☆

RESOURCES

Regional Centers help people who have a developmental disability and their families to find services. They can refer you to programs in your area that may need volunteers (you'll need to explain what kind of organization you're looking for).

❖ Regional Center of the East Bay: Alameda County and Contra Costa County (ask for Communications and Training Unit), (510) 451-7232

❖ Golden Gate Regional Center (ask for Intake and Referral): San Francisco County, (415) 546-9222; Marin County, (415) 945-1600; San Mateo County, (415) 574-9232

❖ North Bay Regional Center: Sonoma, Napa, and Solano counties, (707) 935-1239, ext. 512

❖ San Andreas Regional Center: Santa Clara, Santa Cruz, and Monterey counties (ask for the Director of Community Services), (408) 374-9960

Tips &

Resources

FINDING A VOLUNTEER JOB

T here are plenty of ways to find organizations in your community that need volunteers. Here are several suggestions, in addition to the resources listed in this book. But don't feel you need to try them all—getting a good volunteer job might be as simple as making a call to your local Volunteer Center.

PLACES TO LOOK

1. A Volunteer Center. Volunteer Centers act as connections between potential volunteers and local agencies or nonprofits that need volunteers. They keep a current list of volunteer openings in each county and can refer you to agencies on the phone, send listings in the mail, or meet with you in person to help you pick a job. (See p. 129 to find the center nearest you.)

2. The phone book. All Bay Area yellow pages include a section at the beginning called "Community Services." This list of organizations is by no means comprehensive, but it's an easy place to start. You'll also find groups listed under headings like Social Services, Family Services, and Environmental Organizations.

3. The library. You'll find useful resources in the reference section. Look for:

❖ Standard reference books like the *Encyclopedia of Associations* (look for the Western Regional Edition) and the *Guide to California Foundations.*

❖ Listings of local service agencies. For example, the Berkeley Public Library has a directory of hundreds of Human Services organizations in Alameda County called *The Big Blue Book*, as well as a computer database called BIN (Berkeley Information Network) with information on more than 3,000 local agencies, nonprofits, clubs, etc.

4. The *United Way Help Guide*. This is a free directory to Bay Area charities. To get a copy, call the I & R Help Link, (415) 772-HELP or (800) 273-6222.

5. A religious group. Most churches, synagogues, mosques, etc., work closely with community organizations or have their own programs to help people in need. They are usually happy to provide information whether you're a member of their congregation or not.

6. Your friends. If you know someone who's currently volunteering, or has in the past, talk to them about it.

7. Your employer. Many Bay Area corporations have volunteer programs for employees. Some even allow employees to volunteer on company time.

8. A professional association. If you're interested in contributing professional skills on a pro bono basis, contact a trade association, union, or other professional group. Many of these groups will keep your name for referral to a nonprofit or individual who needs help.

9. A local college or university. Many Bay Area colleges and universities list volunteer opportunities. For example, San Francisco State has a Community Involvement Center, and U.C. Berkeley helps students find volunteer work through their Cal Volunteer Corps. In most cases, these groups make their resources available to the general public as well as to students.

10. The newspaper. Many newspapers list volunteer Help Wanted ads in their classified section. Check out community papers, alternative weeklies, college papers, etc., as well as the major dailies.

11. The World Wide Web. Try Impact Online at (http://www.impactonline.org), the Bay Area Volunteer Information Center at (http://www.meer.net/users/taylor/) or the Volunteer Center of San Francisco at (http://www.volunteercentersf.org).

CHOOSING THE RIGHT JOB

Once you've found a few organizations you might want to work with, the next step is to learn more about them and find out what they need. To save time, you can get basic information over the phone, then decide if it's worth visiting in person.

1. MAKE SOME PHONE CALLS

• When you call an organization, ask for the Volunteer Coordinator. If they don't have one, tell whoever answers the phone that you're considering volunteering. They'll connect you with the right person. In a pinch, you can ask for the "Director."

• Don't feel slighted if your call isn't returned immediately. *That doesn't mean they don't need volunteers.* Many of these groups are short-staffed...or the staff may be involved in crisis situations that take priority.

• "Be persistent," says Suzan Bateson of the Volunteer Center of Contra Costa. "Give it a few days. Then, if you haven't heard back, call again. Sometimes the Volunteer Coordinator is only in one or two days a week."

2. ASK QUESTIONS

• Organizations that seem similar can actually be quite different in their approach. For example, some soup kitchens serve hundreds of people, while others serve only a few and emphasize creating an atmosphere of hospitality. It's important to understand the philosophy of an organization and be sure you feel comfortable with it. Ask them to send you a brochure if they have one. If not, here are some questions to ask:

❖ What does your organization do?

❖ Who do you serve? (People in a certain area, age group, etc.)

❖ Do you have a specific philosophy guiding your work?

- It's also important to understand a group's philosophy on volunteers. Some use volunteers only for particular jobs...others are *run* by volunteers. If you're looking for a chance to implement your own ideas, you'll be happier in a place where you're allowed more freedom. Ask:
    - ❖ How many volunteers are there in your group?
    - ❖ What are their responsibilities?
    - ❖ Can you describe the people who volunteer? Is there anything they have in common? (e.g., Are they all over 60? All women? All interested in politics?)
- Finally, find out if the organization has openings for volunteers or has current projects they need help with. If an opening sounds interesting, ask:
    - ❖ What does the job entail?
    - ❖ What skills or qualifications are needed?
    - ❖ How much training is involved?
    - ❖ Is there a time commitment?

Note: You may be surprised to come across a group that actually has a waiting list for volunteers. Remember, just because a particular program is at capacity right now doesn't mean you aren't badly needed...*somewhere*. Keep looking!

3. SCHEDULE AN INTERVIEW

- Before you make your final choice, consider paying a visit. There's some information you can only get face-to-face, such as whether you like the overall environment and the people.

- Schedule an appointment with the Volunteer Coordinator (or another appropriate person) or attend a group orientation session. Plan on spending at least an hour looking around and talking to people. Keep notes, so you can compare jobs later.

4. PAY A VISIT

- When you arrive for your interview, you may be given a job application to fill out. Don't be put off by this. Though volunteer jobs don't involve money, they can involve a lot of responsibility. Applications help organizations to screen out people who aren't qualified or aren't prepared to take the job seriously.

- If you have a specific job in mind, this is your chance to find out more about what the work is like, what your responsibilities will be, and what the challenges and rewards of the job are.

- You can also ask about what's important to you: "Will I be working with other people?" "Will I learn to use the computer?" "Will I get to know some of the children here?" "How much will I be working outdoors?"

- It helps to talk to other volunteers who are doing the same job or have done it in the past. If no one's available while you're there, ask the Volunteer Coordinator to have someone call you at their convenience.

- If you're still not sure whether the job is right for you, see if you can "shadow" another volunteer for an hour or two.

- "Remember, it's okay to explore...to talk to as many people as you want, with no strings attached," says Tina Cheplick of the Volunteer Center of Marin. "Most agencies understand."

- It's also okay to negotiate. Sometimes a job is *almost* right, but not quite. If that happens, talk with the Volunteer Coordinator. "Volunteers have more leeway than they think," says Donna Campbell of the Volunteer Center of Alameda County. "Come back with an alternative. Say, 'I'm really committed to what you're doing, but I'm looking for X, Y, Z. Is that possible?'"

CREATING YOUR OWN PROJECT

- If you have special skills that you want to use as a volunteer, it may make more sense to design your own project than to take an already-defined job. It takes more initiative, but it's a good chance to be creative.

- For example, if you're a writer or an editor, you could create a newsletter for an organization that doesn't have one...if you're a carpenter, you might want to build new kitchen cupboards for a homeless shelter...an organizational expert could design a new filing system for a nonprofit...and so on.

- Schedule a brainstorming meeting with the Volunteer Coordinator or Director, agree on a project, and write a brief proposal. Include what you want to do and the specific things you've discussed—e.g., deadlines, who pays for materials, etc.

MAKING IT WORK

Here are 10 things that will help make your
volunteer experience a good one.

1. MAKE IT A COMMITMENT

• "Treat your volunteer work like a regular job," says Cathy Maupin of the Volunteer Center of San Mateo. "Get there on time, and if you can't be there, call and let someone know. Show the people you're working with that they can count on you. You'll be a lot more effective in the work that you do."

• Even if there's no time commitment required for the job, it's a good idea to make one to yourself. "Three months is reasonable," says Donna Campbell of the Volunteer Center of Alameda County. "After that, if you don't feel good about the job, it's probably not right for you. But until you've given it that time, you really don't know."

• Once you start, give yourself time to get comfortable. It takes longer to reach a comfort level with volunteer work than it does when you're starting a new job or starting school, because you may only go for a couple hours a week.

2. GET A JOB DESCRIPTION

Unless your job is extremely simple, it's a good idea to ask your supervisor for a written job description. "Some groups will be very clear about your job duties," explains Cathy Maupin. "But others have a habit of saying 'just do whatever you want.' Getting a job description is a way to avoid misunderstandings. It doesn't have to be formal. Even just having a conversation about it helps. You just want to be sure both parties expect the same thing."

3. ASK FOR FEEDBACK

• In most regular jobs, you'd expect feedback on your work. But in the volunteer world, that doesn't always happen. The staff may be so overwhelmed with work or so grateful to have help that it doesn't occur to them to find ways to make you more effective.

• "If you're not getting as much guidance—or appreciation—as you feel you need, you may just have to ask 'How am I doing?,' " says Suzan Bateson of the Volunteer Center of Contra Costa County. "Sometimes that's hard for volunteers. They tell themselves 'I'm here to give, not to receive...I shouldn't need anything.' But that's not true. You shouldn't feel uncomfortable about needing feedback. Everyone does."

4. BE AWARE OF YOUR OWN BOUNDARIES

• If you work directly with people in need—sick children, homebound seniors, the homeless, people with AIDS—you're probably not afraid of "getting involved." Maybe you're looking forward to it. But it's important to think about *how* involved you want to get.

• For example, imagine you're tutoring a group of troubled teenagers in a classroom. As time goes by, you get to know one or two of your students on a more personal level and want to see them outside of class, too—maybe take them to a museum or out to dinner—and become more of a mentor in their lives. Should you?

• Imagine possible scenarios. How would this change your relationship? Do you really have additional time to give...or would getting more involved interfere with your work or family life? Would you feel comfortable having these kids call you at home?

• "Don't feel guilty about deciding what you want to do and what you don't want to do," adds Suzan Bateson. "And then find a way to communicate that to the other people involved so their expectations will be realistic."

• It may also be a good idea to talk over boundary issues and guidelines with your supervisor. Ask in advance what issues are likely to come up and how other people have handled them.

5. CREATE A SUPPORT SYSTEM

• Volunteering can be a very challenging and emotional experience. It's good to have someone to talk to, whether it's other volunteers, or friends who'll listen to your feelings and share your enthusiasm, your questions, your ups and downs.

• "Having a support system increases your satisfaction with your work," says Donna Campbell, "It gives you an chance to reflect on what you're doing and work through any issues that come up."

• Organized support groups are part of many volunteer programs. Ask your Volunteer Coordinator if there is a group meeting at your organization. If not, you can form one on your own. Ask other volunteers if they would be interested or put a flyer up on the organization's bulletin board.

6. EXPECT AN ADJUSTMENT

• If you're coming from a business background or are used to getting things done quickly and efficiently, working with a nonprofit may be frustrating for you. No matter how important their work is, they may not have enough money or staff...and things may move at a much slower pace than you're used to.

• "On the positive side," says Tina Cheplick, "nonprofits are often more creative and are less likely to say something 'can't be done.' It's a trade-off."

7. BE REALISTIC

• Of course you want your work to have an impact, but if your expectations are unrealistic, they can get in your way.

• One way to set your expectations at a realistic level is to talk to your supervisor about them beforehand. Get a sense of what kind of results you can expect and on what kind of timetable.

• "Tutoring kids is the perfect example of the need for patience in volunteering," says Suzan Bateson. "Success comes one small step at a time. In some cases, you may never see the difference you've made in that child's life. But there could come a day, even years later, when something you did or said becomes very important to them. It's like planting a seed; you never know when it will come up. If you accept that going in, you'll enjoy the work a lot more."

8. PACE YOURSELF

• Trying to do too much can be self-defeating. "Too often we think that what is worth doing is worth overdoing," says Douglas M. Lawson, author of *Give to Live*. "That can lead to disillusionment.... The best counsel I know is 'take small bites'.... Start slow, be aware of your energy level, and take your time."

• Even when your volunteer work is at a manageable level, something may come up in your life that requires you to make a change. "If your family or your career...demand attention... protect yourself," says Lawson. "Back away from your volunteer work until you meet your more basic commitments. It is absolutely appropriate to step back when family or work crises arise....There is no loss of integrity in such a move. Your goal [as a volunteer] is to advance the cause you believe in and enhance your life. You can't do either if you're overcommitted."

9. IF IT DOESN'T WORK OUT...

• If, despite your best intentions, you end up with a volunteer job that isn't suited to you or is just a bad situation—and there's nothing else you'd like to do at that organization—simply fulfill your most immediate obligation, then let your supervisor know that you won't be coming back and explain why.

• "Don't be a martyr," says Cathy Maupin. "You should expect to enjoy the work most of the time. If you've met the commitment you had in your mind—or the commitment the agency asked for—you should be able to walk away without feeling guilty."

• "When you leave an organization, tell them what happened," adds Donna Campbell. "If you don't feel you can tell them face to face or over the phone, write them a note. And be specific. If you felt like you didn't get enough feedback, say so. They may be able to learn from your experience and improve their program. It's okay to be honest."

10. RECOGNIZE WHEN IT'S TIME TO MOVE ON

• It's possible that your volunteer job will still be an important part of your life five years from now. But people's needs and lives change over time. "Even if you love what you're doing, after a year or two, it may be time for a new experience," says Campbell, "either in the same organization or somewhere else."

• So every few months, review what you're doing to be sure it's still working for you. "Change and challenge keep all of us flexible and involved," writes Douglas Lawson in *Give to Live.* "Moving on to a new volunteer job is not desertion, it's a celebration of your healthy respect for the quality of your own life."

SERVE ON A NONPROFIT BOARD

T here are over 14,000 nonprofit organizations in the Bay Area, and all are governed by a volunteer Board of Directors. Board members come and go, so at any time, many of these agencies are looking for people to serve on their Board.

In general, it is the board members who define the organization's mission and set policies, goals, and budgets. They also hire and review the organization's Executive Director.

Most board members do fundraising for the organization as well. But responsibilities vary; the role each board member plays depends on their skills and interests and the needs of the organization.

• "Though some boards ask that their members have specific qualifications, in general, board members are just ordinary people," explains Katherina Rosqueta of Board Match Plus in San Francisco, an organization that recruits people to serve on nonprofit boards. "They bring a wide range of skills, experience, and resources."

• For many people, serving on aboard is a 'next step' in long volunteer career. "They've been tutors or mentors; they've done beach cleanups or organized fundraising events," says Rosqueta. "Now they want to get involved in at the 'big picture' level."

Getting Started: Most board members put in between five and eight hours a month. They attend a monthly meeting and often serve on committees or take on projects.

• To serve on a Board, find an organization that interests you and let their current Board know that you're interested in joining them when there's an opening.

• These agencies connect people to Bay Area organizations looking for board members: Board Match Plus, in San Francisco, (415) 982-8999, ext. 241/226; The Management Center, in San Francisco,(415) 362-9735; TheBoard Connection, in San Jose, (408) 244-0440.

GROUP VOLUNTEERING

Volunteering with other people can be a lot of fun and a good chance to "get your feet wet" if you've never volunteered before. It's a way to meet new people or to spend more time with friends, while doing something for your community. There are basically two ways to do it: Join a group project that's already organized or plan one of your own.

JOINING A GROUP PROJECT

• This is as easy as it gets. There are organizations in the Bay Area that specialize in group volunteer projects (see p. 124). Call to get on their mailing list. You'll receive a monthly calendar that describes what they're doing, when, and where—from physical jobs like painting playground equipment to helping kids with their homework to serving food in a soup kitchen.

• "We take care of all the details," says George Flemming, director of Hands On San Francisco. "You just pick something that interests you and show up." Volunteer Centers organize group activities, too (see p. 129). Call one to get their current calendar.

PLANNING A GROUP PROJECT

This is more complicated, but it's a great way to get involved if you have a group you want to volunteer with—people at work, a soft-ball team, a church committee, or friends and family. Here's how:

1. Find a project. Your group can: (a) join a project that's already organized by calling one of the programs listed on p. 124; (b) work with a Volunteer Center, which knows the needs of local agencies; (c) look for a one-time event such as a walk-a-thon or Christmas in April project (see p. 132 for more ideas); or (d) contact a nonprofit on your own.

• If someone in your group is already volunteering with a particular program, you might start there. "Ask if they need something done that could use a concentration of people power," advises Tina Cheplick of the Marin Volunteer Center. "But be sure the project fulfills a real need and isn't just something created for your group.

People won't feel as good about doing 'make-work' as they will about doing something important."

2. Plan ahead. Here are a few tips:

• "Start thirty to sixty days in advance," says Suzan Bateson of the Volunteer Center of Contra Costa. "That way your friends will have plenty of time to line up babysitting, etc., and you can set things up with the organization."

• Once you've picked a project, decide on the size of the group and the date, then send out invitations. "One option is to ask three people, and then each of you find two more people," says Cheplick. "That gives you a group of twelve, which is a nice size. The larger the group, the more organization is involved. We have an annual group-volunteering event on Mt. Tamalpais. We usually have about a hundred people, and it takes *four months* of planning."

• Ask people to RSVP by a certain date. That way you can tell the organization how many are coming. "Expect a few no-shows," advises Bateson. "Usually ten to twenty percent." In your invitation, mention that people who can't come can contribute in other ways—for example, by providing refreshments.

• As the coordinator, it's your job to communicate with the agency, make sure everyone in your group knows what to do, and make sure that the organization's needs, as well as your needs (as a group) are met. For example, if this is a way for people in your group to get to know each other, you might plan to have coffee before you start working and take a group picture.

3. Follow through. When your group is finished with the volunteer project, talk to the organization about how things went and find out what their needs are for the future. Do they have more projects for groups? Do they need volunteers who can come weekly? "If you pass on this information to the group, with a contact name, you'll be doing the organization an additional service," says Cheplick.

GROUP VOLUNTEERING ORGANIZATIONS

Hands On San Francisco, (415) 281-9953; **Oakland Cares,** (510) 465-7935; **Community Impact** in Menlo Park (organizes projects all around the Bay Area), (415) 323-7131.

VOLUNTEERING THROUGH RELIGIOUS GROUPS

Religious groups run a large range of programs and services in the Bay Area. If you follow a religion or consider yourself to be a spiritual person, this could be the perfect way for you to volunteer.

"Doing charitable work...'honoring your neighbor'...is a primary teaching in most religions," explains Dwayne Marsh of the Bay Area FAITHS Initiative. "The work becomes an expression of faith—as well as an effort to make your community a better place to live."

WHAT RELIGIOUS GROUPS ARE DOING

Religious groups serve local communities in just about every way: They're major financial contributors to community organizations, they offer groups use of their facilities, and they do *all* the things discussed in this book—from working with kids to protecting the environment. What each congregation does depends on local needs, its size, and what's important to members. Some examples:

- ❖ The Buena Vista United Methodist Church in Alameda sponsors an interfaith basketball league for kids.
- ❖ In addition to serving over 3,000 free meals a day, Glide Memorial Church in San Francisco administers more than 35 social service and advocacy programs.
- ❖ The Islamic Information and Education Center in San Jose sponsors projects that promote understanding between Muslims and Jews.
- ❖ The Zen Center of San Francisco runs a hospice.
- ❖ The Marin Interfaith Council hosts an ethnic theater production followed by a discussion of how differences enrich our lives.
- ❖ Congregation Beth Am in Palo Alto provides food, clothing, and counseling to people who are homeless.

DIFFERENT TYPES OF RELIGIOUS GROUPS

- **Congregations** traditionally divide volunteer work into two types: "religious volunteering" (helping to run the church or temple or coordinate events) and "nonreligious volunteering" (helping in the general community). *Note:* You usually don't have to be a member of a congregation to take part in its volunteer programs.

- **Denominational groups** connected to a particular faith (Jewish Vocational Services, Catholic Charities, and the Episcopal Sanctuary, for example) serve the general public and welcome people of all faiths as volunteers.

- **Interfaith groups** represent a number of faiths and congregations. They're usually based in a geographic area and work on projects that benefit the entire community. Their focus is bringing people of different faiths together.

Where to Look. Churches are listed in the yellow pages (by denomination), as are Synagogues. Ask the pastor, rabbi, or Volunteer Coordinator about volunteer work. You can also learn about volunteer opportunities by reading the newsletter or bulletin, or paying special attention during announcement time at services.

- To find denominational groups, check the yellow pages under Religious Organizations or call a Volunteer Center (see p. 129).

- There's at least one interfaith group in every county. You can find them in the yellow pages under Religious Organizations. Or call the FAITHS Initiative, (415) 495-3100, an umbrella organization that represents religious groups throughout the Bay Area.

SPIRITUALITY AND VOLUNTEERING

- The difference between getting involved through a religious group and volunteering with a secular nonprofit is often subtle. In an interfaith group, for example, there may be little said that is explicitly religious. In other groups, volunteers pray and reflect on their work together, as a way to deepen their faith.

- One thing you can count on is an atmosphere where faith is welcome. "We're the social service arm of the Catholic church; that's our focus, not religion," says Irma Dillard with Catholic Charities of San Francisco. "But our programs are based on Christian values, and if religion comes up in our work, we're free to talk about it. There's an openness to religious feeling here that doesn't necessarily exist in nonreligious nonprofits."

ADVOCACY

P art of playing an active role in your community is making sure your voice is heard on public policy issues. It's another way to support the groups or institutions (schools, libraries, parks, etc.) you feel are important.

Of course it's important to vote. But you can also work directly for community groups, collecting signatures on ballot petitions, assisting with mailings or newsletters, writing letters to newspapers or politicians, etc. The amount of work you do is up to you—you can put in a few hours making phone calls or organize a whole campaign.

Examples of issues that need support:

• **Libraries.** All over the Bay Area, libraries threatened with budget cuts have been saved by community support. Call your local library or Friends of the Library group (see p. 100) to find out the status of their funding. Let them know you'd like to help if they mount a campaign.

• **AIDS.** If you feel government should do more to address the AIDS crisis, you can help by joining an AIDS advocacy group such as HIV Advocacy Network (HAN), (415) 487-3034; San Mateo County AIDS office, (415) 573-2030; Marin AIDS Advisory Commission, (415) 499-7804; East Bay AIDS Foundation, (510) 433-1000; or Sonoma County AIDS Foundation, (707) 544-1215.

• **Seniors.** "There are issues of importance to seniors being voted on all the time," says Lilian Rabinovitz, a volunteer with the Gray Panthers in Berkeley. "We're working on national health care, making public transportation more accessible, and improving licensing requirements for nursing homes, to name a few." To find senior advocacy groups, call an Area Agency on Aging (see p. 51).

• **Children.** When budgets get tight, community services for children—soccer leagues, summer camps, youth employment programs, etc.—are often cut back or eliminated altogether. To find out how you can be an advocate for children's services, call Coleman Advocates in San Francisco, (415) 641-4362, or Children Now in Oakland, (510) 763-2444 or (800) CHILD-44.

CITY/COUNTY VOLUNTEER CONTACTS

Some Bay Area cities and counties have volunteer programs that recruit local citizens. Each program is different. Some primarily maintain parks and other outdoor areas. Some need people to help in summer day camps. Others focus on crime prevention. If your city or county is on this list, you can give them a call to find out what their needs are. If not, you can still volunteer with parks, police departments, etc., by calling them directly.

City of Campbell
(408) 966-2198

County of Contra Costa
(510) 313-7910

City of Cupertino
(408) 252-4505

Town of Danville
(510) 820-6074

City of East Palo Alto
(415) 853-3127

Town of Fairfax
(415) 453-4532

City of Fairfield
(707) 428-7589 or -7767

City of Fremont
(510) 494-4543

City of Gilroy
(408) 848-0460

City of Hayward
(510) 888-0102

City of Los Altos
(415) 948-1491, ext. 229

County of Marin
(415) 499-6104

City of Milpitas
(408) 842-2470

City of Morgan Hill
(408) 779-3033

City of Mountain View
(415) 903-6607

City of Palo Alto
(415) 329-2189

Town of San Anselmo
(415) 258-4676

City of San Leandro
(510) 577-3463

City of San Rafael
(415) 485-3407

City of Santa Clara
(408) 984-3165

County of Santa Clara
(408) 441-5755

County of Santa Cruz
(408) 454-2987

City of Saratoga
(408) 867-3438, ext. 252

County of Sonoma
(707) 527-2317 or -2335

City of Sunnyvale
(408) 730-7533

City of Vacaville
(707) 449-5268

BAY AREA
VOLUNTEER CENTERS

There are eleven Volunteer Centers in the greater Bay Area—basically one in each county. Each keeps a current database of organizations that need volunteers. If you call a center and explain what kind of volunteer work you're looking for, they will refer you to a nearby program. If you're not sure what you'd like to do, most centers will mail you a list of volunteer opportunities or meet with you and help you decide.

Volunteer Center of San Francisco County
1160 Battery Street, Suite 70, San Francisco 94111
Phone: (415) 982-8999   Fax: (415) 399-9214
Web site: *http://www.volunteercentersf.org*
E-mail: volctrsf@aol.com

Lists about 1,500 volunteer opportunities. Publishes quarterly listings, holiday and special event directories, and guides to youth volunteering. Runs special programs including vocationally oriented volunteering for people with disabilities, professional development through community involvement for corporate employees, and training and placement of diverse individuals on nonprofit boards. Runs volunteer Help Wanted ads in eight community newspapers.

Volunteer Center of Alameda County
1904 Franklin Street, Suite 211, Oakland 94612
Phone: (510) 419-3970   Fax: (510) 419-3975
Hayward,   (510) 538-0554; Pleasanton, (510) 462-3570

Lists about 1,600 volunteer opportunities. Publishes "Agency Link," a bimonthly bulletin for nonprofits listing volunteer management resources and workshops, and a Corporate Bulletin of East Bay evening and weekend volunteering.

Volunteer Center of Contra Costa
1820 Bonanza Street, Suite 100, Walnut Creek 94596
Phone: (510) 472-5760   Fax: (510) 472-5780

Lists about 600 volunteer opportunities. Has a monthly calendar of one-time jobs, and a monthly list of projects for youth volunteers. Also coordinates a holiday program that provides gifts and food for people in need. Runs volunteer Help Wanted ads in the *Contra Costa Times*, *Post Dispatch*, and other papers.

Volunteer Center of Marin County
650 Las Gallinas, San Rafael 94903
Phone: (415) 479-5660   Fax: (415) 479-9722

Lists 300 to 350 volunteer opportunities. Offers a monthly calendar of one-time jobs and materials for young volunteers and families who want to volunteer together. Also recruits board members for over 100 local nonprofits. Lists volunteer Help Wanted ads in the *Marin Independent Journal* and local weeklies.

Volunteer Center of Napa County
1820 Jefferson Street, Napa 94559
Phone: (707) 252-6222   Fax: (707) 226-5179

Lists about 150 volunteer opportunities. In addition to a database, has several programs of its own, including a van that provides transportation for elderly and disabled people, and a senior visiting program. Lists volunteer Help Wanted ads in the *Napa Register*, *Weekly Calistogan*, and other local papers.

Volunteer Center of San Mateo County
800 South Claremont, Suite 108, San Mateo 94402
Phone: (415) 342-0801   Fax: (415) 342-1399

Lists about 800 volunteer opportunities. Offers a quarterly calendar of one-time jobs and a Youth Directory of volunteer jobs. Runs volunteer Help Wanted ads in local papers, including the *San Mateo Times* and *SF Weekly*.

Volunteer Exchange of Santa Clara County
1922 The Alameda, Suite 211, San Jose 95126
Phone: (408) 247-1126   Fax: (408) 247-5805
North county: (415) 965-2426; South county: (408) 683-4061

Lists 1,300 to 1,400 volunteer opportunities. Offers a monthly bulletin of short-term opportunities, an updated list of youth volunteer jobs three times a year, and a November newsletter listing hundreds of holiday volunteer jobs. Volunteer opportunities are also listed on the *San Jose Mercury News* online network.

Volunteer Center of Solano County
505 Santa Clara Street, Vallejo 94590
Phone: (707) 645-7899

Lists about 80 volunteer opportunities. Sponsors the Human Race, a walk-a-thon fundraiser for local nonprofits held every May. Runs volunteer Help Wanted ads in the *Daily Republic*.

Volunteer Center of Sonoma County
1041 Fourth Street, Santa Rosa CA 95404
Phone: (707) 573-3399 Fax: (707) 573-3380
Petaluma, (707) 762-0111; Sonoma, (707) 996-4664; Rohnert Park, (707) 588-9690.

Lists about 600 volunteer opportunities. Offers a Youth Resource Guide and a monthly "spot job" bulletin for companies with volunteer programs. Also recruits board members for over 80 local nonprofits and publishes an annual Directory of Human Service Agencies listing 700 programs.

Volunteer Center of Santa Cruz County
1010 Emeline Avenue, Santa Cruz CA 94060
Phone: (408) 423-0554 Fax: (408) 423-6267
Watsonville, (408) 722-6708; San Lorenzo Valley, (408) 335-6844
Web site: *http://www.infopoint.com/sc/orgs/VOLUNTEER CENTER*

Lists about 600 volunteer opportunities in nonprofits, schools, and local government. Publishes a monthly column in the *Santa Cruz County Sentinel*, youth opportunities, and a Teacher Guide to Youth Services. Runs 16 volunteer-based programs. Sponsors Making a Difference Day in the fall.

Volunteer Center of Monterey County
801 Lighthouse Avenue, Monterey CA 93940
Phone: (800) 776-9176 Fax: (408) 655-4326
Web site: *http:/bbs.ci.seaside.ca.us/vol/home.htm*

Lists about 2,000 volunteer opportunities countywide. Publishes weekly column in the *Monterey County Herald* and other local newspapers outlining opportunities. Sponsors the Human Race in the spring. Branch in Salinas.

OTHER ORGANIZATIONS

- **United Way of the Bay Area.** County offices: Alameda, (510) 238-2410; Contra Costa, (510) 686-4186; Marin, (415) 492-9840; San Francisco, (415) 772-4401; San Mateo, (415) 345-4871. **United Way of Santa Clara County:** (408) 247-1200. **United Way of Santa Cruz County:** (408)-479-5466. **Monterey Peninsula United Way:** (408) 372-8026. **Napa-Solano United Way:** (707) 644-4131. **United Way of Sonoma-Mendocino-Lake:** (707) 528-4483.

- **Retired Senior Volunteer Program (RSVP).** A federal volunteer program for people over 55. For information, call (800) 424-8867.

- **American Association of Retired Persons (AARP).** AARP runs a number of volunteer-based programs. For info, call the California state office, (916) 446-2277.

- **The Volunteerism Project.** A nonprofit devoted to strengthening and diversifying volunteerism in the Bay Area. Call (415) 772-7393.

SELECTED JOBS

*We've selected just 10 volunteer jobs for each category (except Animals).
There are lots more ideas in the What You Can Do section.*

One-Time Opportunities

Sort food in a food bank, p.38
Visit a senior at holiday time, p.48
Join the S.F. AIDS Walk-a-thon, p.53
Give a talk at a school, p.64
Help Christmas in April, p. 80
Usher at a performance, p. 84 or 86
Answer pledge-drive calls, p.87
Give blood, p. 91
Work in a neighborhood park, p.95
Help at a library book sale
   or event, p.102
Also see Outdoor Opportunities

Things Families Can Do Together

Organize a food drive, p.38
Pick fruits and vegetables, p.40
Make a neighborhood map, p.42
Visit a senior at holiday time, p.48
Help an older person at home, p.48
Adopt a family in need, p.79
Clean-up a creek or beach, p.58 or 60
Raise money for a school, p.66
Work in a neighborhood park, p.95
Raise a guide dog puppy, p.110

Opportunities for Seniors

Further Reading:

*Golden Opportunities: A Volunteer
Guide for Americans Over 50* by Andy
Carroll. (Peterson's Guides, 1994)

Become an ombudsman
   for the elderly, p.46
Give a talk at a school, p.64
Teach something you know, p.65
Tutor students, p.65
Work in a museum
   or gallery, p. 83 or 84

Answer pledge-drive calls, p.87
Work in a hospital, p.89
Join a local park group, p.95
Support a community garden, p.96
Help a library, pp. 101-103

Projects for Groups

Sort food in a food bank, p.38
Join the S.F. AIDS Walk-a-thon,
   p.53
Clean up a creek or beach,
   p.58 or 60
Raise money for a school, p.66
Work with Habitat for
   Humanity, p.79
Help Christmas in April, p.80
Answer pledge-drive calls, p.87
Work in a neighborhood park, p.95
Do trail maintenance, p.96
Help at a Special
   Olympics event, p.107

Outdoor Opportunities

Go on a wilderness trip for
   city kids, p.34
Pick fruit and vegetables, p.40
Garden in the AIDS Grove, p.53
Protect the Bay: stencil drains, p. 58
Clean a creek or beach, p.58 or 60.
Pull out exotic plants, p.60
Work in a local park, p.95
Support a community garden, p.96
Patrol a trail while you hike or do
   trail maintenance, p.96
Become a park docent, p.98

Working with Animals

Work in a wildlife hospital, p. 62
Help abandoned animals, p. 62
Raise a guide dog puppy, p. 110